Claire Collins

Claire Collins

WHERE IS IT?

QUESTION & ANSWER
ENCYCLOPEDIA

WHERE IS IT?

General Editor   Lesley Firth

KINGFISHER BOOKS

First published in 1984 by Kingfisher Books Limited
Elsley Court, 20-22 Great Titchfield Street
London W1P 7AD
A Grisewood & Dempsey Company

BRITISH LIBRARY CATALOGUING IN PUBLICATION DATA

Question and answer encyclopedia — Where is it?
    1. Children's encyclopedias and dictionaries
    I, Firth, Lesley
    032   AG5
    ISBN 0 86272 122 9
    D. L. TO: 980-1984

Phototypeset by Crawley Composition
Colour separations by Newsele Litho Ltd,
Milan, Italy
Printed in Spain by Artes Gráficas Toledo, S.A.

Authors
David Lambert
Mark Lambert
Brian Williams
Jill Wright

Artists
Bob Bampton/The Garden Studio
Norma Burgin/John Martin & Artists
Oliver Frey/Temple Art Agency
Bernard Robinson/Tudor Art Studios
Mike Roffe
Mike Saunders/Jillian Burgess
Trevor Scobie/John Martin & Artists
Tammy Wong/John Martin & Artists

CONTENTS

PLANET EARTH

Where is the Greenwich Meridian?   10
Where can you see the Sun at midnight?   10
Where is the magnetic North Pole?   10
Where could you have a foot in Thursday and
   a foot in Friday?   11
Where is the horizon?   11

Where is the Earth's crust being formed?   12
Where is the Earth's crust being destroyed?   12
Where is the San Andreas fault?   13
Where is the Great Rift Valley?   13
Where will the continents be in another
   50 million years?   13

Where are the oldest rocks?   14
Where can you see over 1500 million years of
   rock strata?   14
Where do crystals form?   15
Where are diamonds found?   15
Where are the best places to look for gold?   15

Where is the world's greatest mountain range?   16
Where is the world's highest mountain?   16
Where is the largest active volcano?   16
Where has a volcano given birth to an island?   17
Where was the biggest volcanic eruption?   17

Which volcano destroyed an ancient Roman
   town?   18
Where is the Pacific 'ring of fire'?   18
Where have the strongest earthquakes
   occurred?   18
Where does mud boil?   19
Where is the epicentre of an earthquake?   19

Where are the world's hottest places?   20
Where are the world's coldest places?   20
Where does frost come from?   20
Where are the wettest places on Earth?   21
Where is the driest place on Earth?   21

Where are the world's longest glaciers?   22
Where are the world's biggest expanses of ice?   22
Where is permafrost found?   22
Where are the biggest icebergs found?   23
Where do icebergs melt?   23
Where are crevasses found?   23

Where is the greatest ocean current?   24
Where are the Doldrums?   24
Where is the Gulf Stream?   24
Where is the abyssal plain?   25
Where is the deepest part of the ocean?   25
Which sea is the saltiest?   25

Where is the largest archipelago?   26
Where do tidal bores occur?   26
Where are the world's highest tides?   26
Where is the longest reef in the world?   27
Where are fiords found?   27

Which is the longest river?   28
Which is the largest river?   28
Where are the highest waterfalls?   28
Where were the worst floods recorded?   29
Where is the largest lake?   29
Where is the highest lake?   29

Where is the biggest cave?   30
Where is the deepest cave?   30
Where are the largest stalactites and
   stalagmites?   30
Where are the largest sand dunes?   31
Where is artesian water found?   31
Where are deserts being created?   31

Where has land reclamation doubled the size
   of a country?   32
Where is the remotest place on Earth?   32
Where is the largest artificial lake?   33
Where is the biggest man-made hole on Earth?   33
Where does acid rain occur?   33

Where is rice grown?   34
Where does cotton come from?   34
Where is tea grown?   34
Where does rubber come from?   35
Where was maize first grown?   35
Where does cocoa come from?   35

Where is Monument Valley? 36
Where is there snow near the Equator? 36
Where is the Giant's Causeway? 37
Where is Wave Rock? 37
Where is 'Old Faithful'? 37

PLANTS AND ANIMALS

Where and what are biomes? 38
Why are some animals found only in certain regions? 39

Where do penguins breed? 40
Which seals live in the Antarctic? 40
Where are polar bears found? 41
Which birds nest in the Arctic? 41
Where do caribou live? 41

Where are bighorn sheep found? 42
Where do ibexes live? 42
Where does the yak live? 42
Where do pandas live? 43
Where do llamas live? 43
Where are the strangest mountain plants found? 43

Where do most conifers grow? 44
Which birds live in coniferous forests? 45
Which mammals live in coniferous forests? 45

Why is deciduous woodland so rich in wildlife? 46
Which animals live in deciduous forests? 46
Which birds live in deciduous forests? 46

Where do coyotes live? 48
Where do prairie dogs make their homes? 48
What happened to the bison? 48
Where does the viscacha live? 49
Why do so few trees grow on grassland? 49

What is savannah? 50
Which birds live in the savannah? 50
Which savannah animals live in herds? 50
Which are the savannah hunters? 51
How do so many animals live together in the savannah? 51
Where is the desert cold in winter? 52
Can fish survive in hot water? 52
Where do cacti grow? 52
Which is the world's largest desert? 53
How do desert animals survive? 53

Where is the world's largest rain forest? 54
Which kinds of bird live in rain forest? 54
Which mammals live in the Amazon rain forest? 55
Which mammals live in African rain forests? 55

Where do flying lemurs live? 56
Where do tigers and rhinoceroses live? 56
Where are mangrove forests found? 57
Where is the home of the orang-utan? 57

Where do birds of paradise live? 58
Where are Banksias found? 58
What do marsupials eat? 59

How many kinds of Hawaiian honeycreeper are there? 60
Why are island animals different from others? 60
Which animals live in the Galapagos Islands? 60
Where are most flightless birds found? 61
Where do crabs climb trees? 61

Why do birds migrate? 62
Where do shearwaters migrate to? 62
Why do whales migrate? 62
Where do monarch butterflies migrate to? 63
Where do green turtles lay their eggs? 63
Where do eels breed? 63

THE PAST

Where were the oldest human footprints found? 64
Where did farmers first grow crops? 64
Where were wheeled carts first used? 65
Where did people first use writing? 65
Where was paper first made? 65

Where was silk first produced? 66
Where was the potter's wheel invented? 66
Where were the first Olympic Games held? 66
Where did the Greeks found colonies? 67
When did people first use money? 67
Where were roads first paved? 67

Where was the plough invented? 68
Where were animals first used for farm work? 68
Where did the first key turn in a lock? 68
Where was iron first smelted? 69
Where were iron weapons first used in war? 69
Where were the first rockets fired? 69

Where did houses first have central heating? 70
Where did Alexander lead his army? 70
Where did the Romans build huge aqueducts? 70
Where did the Roman Empire end? 71
Where were the first universities founded? 71
Where has the most ancient Bible been found? 71

Where did Muhammad flee? 72
Which European city was the capital of an
  Islamic empire? 72
Where was Cathay? 72
Where did Europe get spices from in the
  Middle Ages? 73
Where was the first book printed? 73
Where did the longbow prove to be decisive
  in warfare? 73

Where did the American Indians come from? 74
Where was the Songhai Empire? 74
Where was El Dorado supposed to be? 74
Where did the Pilgrim Fathers land? 75
Where did a tea party start a revolution? 75
Where did the Opium War break out? 75

Where did American slaves found a free
  country? 76
Where did the Boxer Rebellion take place? 76
Where did tanks first play a part in warfare? 76
Where did the League of Nations meet? 77
Where were the first atomic bombs dropped? 77
Where was the Six-Day War fought? 77

PEOPLE AND PLACES

Where do people live in tents? 78
Where do people live in wooden houses? 78
Where do people live in houses on stilts? 79
Where do people live in mud houses? 79
Where do people live on boats? 79

Where can Stone-Age people still be found? 80
Where do the Masai live? 80
Where do Bushmen live? 80
Where do Sherpas live? 81
Where do the Ainu live? 81
Where do gypsies come from? 81

Where do aborigines live? 82
Where do Maoris live? 82
Where do the Tuareg live? 82
Where do pygmies live? 83
Where do Eskimos live? 83
Where do Lapps live? 83

Where have ancient temples been dismantled
 and rebuilt? 84
Where is the Valley of the Kings? 84
Where is the biggest Roman amphitheatre? 84
Where were pyramids discovered in the jungle? 85
Where is the lost city of the Incas? 85
Where is Angkor Wat? 85

Which is a holy city for three religions? 86
Where is the Wailing Wall? 86
Where is the centre of the Roman Catholic
 Church? 86
Where is the holy city of the Hindus? 87
Where do Christians make pilgrimage? 87
Where is the biggest statue of Buddha? 87

Which cities are built on canals? 88
Where are the Low Countries? 88
Where is the Black Forest? 88
Where is Versailles? 89
Where are Gothic cathedrals found? 89
Where is Trooping the Colour held? 89

Where is the Ponte Vecchio? 90
Where is the Leaning Tower? 90
Where is the Escorial? 90
Where is the Alhambra? 91
Where is the Kremlin? 91
Where is Red Square? 91

Which great city has had four names? 92
Where is the Krak des Chevaliers? 92
Which are the richest countries in the world? 92
Where is Isfahan? 93
Where is Bangladesh? 93
Where is the Gateway of India? 93

Where is the Taj Mahal? 94
Where is the Golden Pagoda? 94
Where are elephants used as working animals? 94
Which city has 'klongs'? 95
Which Asian city and country share the same
 name? 95
What are Chinese pagodas? 95

Where is taking tea a ceremony? 96
Which is the world's biggest city? 96
Where is Ginza? 96
Where is the Forbidden City? 97
Which country has the largest population? 97
Where do people make gardens from stones? 97

Where can you see a kasbah? 98
Where are souks found? 98
Where is Timbuktu? 98
Where is the largest African national park? 99
Where do people go on safari? 99
Where are the oldest churches in Africa? 99

Where are oases found? 100
Where is the longest big-ship canal? 100
Where was the Benin Empire? 100
Where is Great Zimbabwe? 101
Where do Zulus live? 101
Where are the Victoria Falls? 101

Where is the Statue of Liberty 102
Where is Manhattan? 102
Where is the White House? 102
Where is Cape Canaveral? 103
Where is Disneyland? 103
Where is the longest artificial seaway? 103

Where did the Olmecs live? 104
Where are four American presidents carved
   out of rock? 104
Which city has floating gardens? 104
Where do North American Indians live? 105
Where are totem poles found? 105
Where is Mesa Verde? 105

Where is the Land of Fire? 106
Where do gauchos live? 106
Which is the highest capital city? 106
Where has Brasília been built? 107
Where is the most colourful carnival held? 107

Which country is the world's largest wool
   producer? 108
Where is the Nullarbor Plain? 108
Which is the largest Australian city? 108
Where is Ayers Rock? 109
Where is the Australian 'outback'? 109
Where did the people of the Pacific Islands
   come from? 109

Where is the longest bridge? 110
Which is the largest country? 110
Where is the tallest building? 111
Where is the longest road tunnel? 111
Which is the smallest country? 111

Where were the Seven Wonders of the World? 112
Where is Easter Island? 112

Where is the home of the yeti? 113
Where is the Bermuda Triangle? 113
Where was Atlantis? 113

TRANSPORT

Where are the world's busiest sea lanes? 114
Where are the main oil sea-routes? 114
Where is the world's busiest port? 114
Where do icebreakers operate? 115
Where are the navigation lights on a ship? 115
Where are lighthouses built? 115

Where is the longest railway? 116
Where did the Orient Express travel? 116
Where is the longest road? 117
Where do people use rickshaws? 117
Which city had the first underground
   railway? 117

How high do aircraft travel? 118
Which are the world's largest airports? 118
Which are the busiest air routes? 118
Where did the worst air accident happen? 119
Where and what is a 'black box'? 119
Where can engines be positioned in an
   aircraft? 119

INDEX

INDEX 120

PLANET EARTH

▼ WHERE IS THE GREENWICH MERIDIAN?

A meridian is a line of longitude, an imaginary line on the Earth's surface between the North and South Poles. The Greenwich Meridian is 0° of longitude. It passes through the Royal Observatory at Greenwich, in London, England.

In 1675 the Royal Observatory was founded on a hill above the king's palace at Greenwich. Last century, a new transit telescope was installed to determine time by measuring the passage of stars. The meridian on which the telescope was situated was fixed as 0°. In 1884 this meridian was accepted as the Prime Meridian. All other lines of longitude are measured east or west of Greenwich.

▼ WHERE CAN YOU SEE THE SUN AT MIDNIGHT?

Near the North and South Poles it never gets dark in the summertime. The Sun can be seen all day and all night – unless it is cloudy.

As the diagram shows, the Earth's axis is tilted. In June the North Pole is tilted towards the Sun. As the Earth rotates on its axis, everywhere within the Arctic Circle remains in sunlight. So even at midnight the Sun can be seen above the horizon.

In December, the South Pole is tilted towards the Sun, and it is summer in Antarctica. The Sun can be seen at midnight within the Antarctic Circle. But in December the Sun never rises above the horizon within the Arctic Circle.

▼ WHERE IS THE MAGNETIC NORTH POLE?

A compass needle always points towards the magnetic North Pole. At present it is near Bathurst Island in northern Canada – over 1500 kilometres from the geographic North Pole.

In 1831, James Clark Ross discovered the magnetic North Pole off the Boothia Peninsula in northern Canada.

Today it is 800 kilometres north of this point. The location of the pole is mainly controlled by movements inside the Earth which make our planet into a giant magnet. Over very long periods of time the Earth's magnetic field can reverse, moving magnetic North to Antarctica. This has happened 30 times in the last five million years.

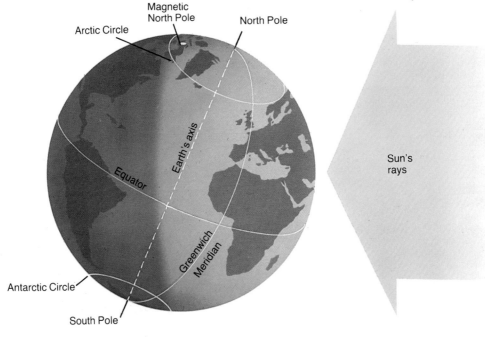

Magnetic North Pole

North Pole

Arctic Circle

Earth's axis

Equator

Greenwich Meridian

Sun's rays

Antarctic Circle

South Pole

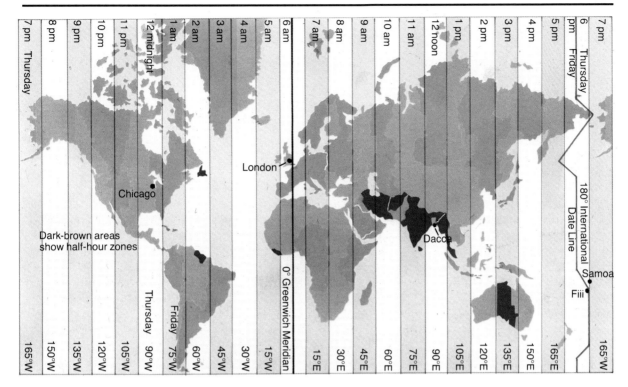

Map labels: 7 pm Thursday | 8 pm | 9 pm | 10 pm | 11 pm | 12 midnight | 1 am | 2 am | 3 am | 4 am | 5 am | 6 am | 7 am | 8 am | 9 am | 10 am | 11 am | 12 noon | 1 pm | 2 pm | 3 pm | 4 pm | 5 pm | 6 pm Friday | 7 pm Thursday Friday

165°W | 150°W | 135°W | 120°W | 105°W | 90°W | 75°W | 60°W | 45°W | 30°W | 15°W | 0° Greenwich Meridian | 15°E | 30°E | 45°E | 60°E | 75°E | 90°E | 105°E | 120°E | 135°E | 150°E | 165°E | 165°W

Chicago · London · Dacca · Samoa · Fiji

180° International Date Line

Thursday | Friday

Dark-brown areas show half-hour zones

▲ WHERE COULD YOU HAVE A FOOT IN THURSDAY AND A FOOT IN FRIDAY?

The date changes at the International Date Line which follows approximately the 180° meridian. This meridian is on the opposite side of the world to the Greenwich Meridian.

The Earth rotates on its axis through 360° in 24 hours. So there is one hour's time difference for every 15° of longitude. Since 1883 the world has been divided into the standard time zones shown on the map.

When the Sun rises on a Friday at 6 a.m. in London (at 0°), it is already midday in Dacca (at 90°E) and it is 6 p.m. on Friday in Fiji (at 180°E). But westwards from London, time is behind Greenwich Mean Time. So when it is 6 a.m. on Friday in London, it is midnight on Thursday in Chicago (90°W). In Samoa (170°W) it is 7 p.m. on Thursday. So when it is Friday evening on the Fijian side of the Date Line, it is Thursday evening on the Samoan side.

▶ WHERE IS THE HORIZON?

The horizon is the boundary where the sky seems to meet the ground or the sea. Because the Earth's surface curves, things seem to disappear over the horizon.

The higher up you are, the further you can see. On a clear day at the seaside you can stand on the beach and watch a boat travel out of sight over the horizon. The curve of the Earth prevents you from seeing it any more. If your eye level is 1.5 metres above sea level, the horizon you can see is 4.5 kilometres away.

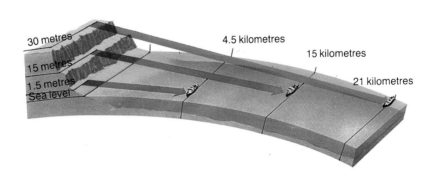

30 metres · 15 metres · 1.5 metres · Sea level · 4.5 kilometres · 15 kilometres · 21 kilometres

If you climb to the top of a cliff, you can see much farther, as the diagram shows. And if you climbed up a mountain to 3000 metres above sea level,

the horizon would be 200 kilometres away – if the weather was good enough to see that far.

New material is added to the Earth's crust by volcanoes. Much of the lava is molten material from the part of the Earth called the mantle which lies beneath the solid crust. Some volcanoes are found on land, but many are located deep beneath the oceans where lava flows onto the seabed.

Imagine an almost round egg with a shell that has been cracked in a number of places.

This is a good picture of our Earth. The Earth's outer layer, the crust, is somewhat similar to the eggshell. It is rigid; it is also very thin when compared to the diameter of the Earth; and it is broken into a number of major and minor parts called crustal plates.

Some crustal plates, such as the Pacific Plate, are made entirely of ocean floor. Many crustal plates include whole continents as well as parts of the ocean floor. These gigantic plates are moving very slowly, and as they move the continents move with them.

In some places the plates are gradually moving apart. As they do so, molten material from beneath the crust wells up and is added to the edges of each crustal plate. Such a boundary is known as a constructive plate margin, and the process of adding new material to each plate is called sea-floor spreading.

The mid-Atlantic Ridge is one of the places where new crust is being formed in this way. The North American and South American Plates are slowly moving away from the Eurasian and African Plates.

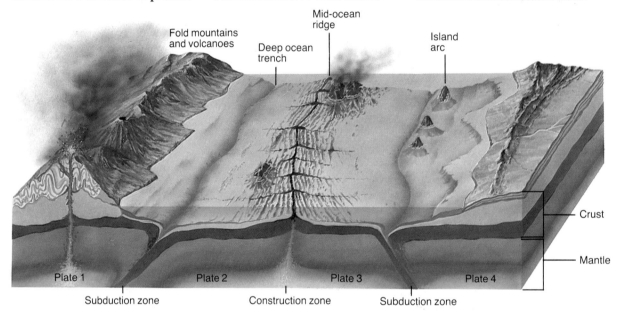

Fold mountains and volcanoes · Deep ocean trench · Mid-ocean ridge · Island arc · Crust · Mantle

Plate 1 · Plate 2 · Plate 3 · Plate 4

Subduction zone · Construction zone · Subduction zone

Most scientists believe that the area of the Earth's surface remains the same. So while material is being added to the crust at the junction of some crustal plates, it is being lost at the junctions of other plates.

As the Atlantic slowly widens, and the Americas move away from Eurasia and Africa, material from the Earth's crust is being lost around the edges of the Pacific Ocean.

The boundaries of the crustal plates at the edge of the Pacific are marked by deep ocean trenches roughly twice as deep as the ocean itself. Scientists now believe that these mark areas where the floor of the Pacific Ocean is being dragged very slowly down under the neighbouring continental plates.

This type of boundary is called a destructive plate margin. The ocean floor is dragged down at an angle towards the mantle. This process is called subduction.

As subduction occurs, the

solid rock melts. This molten material rises through cracks in the rocks above, forming volcanoes. As the crustal plates slide across each other, earthquakes often occur, and the overriding continental crust is folded and pushed up to form mountains.

Recent evidence of activity at a destructive plate margin was the eruption of Mount St Helens in the USA. Mount St Helens is one of an arc of volcanoes caused by the subduction of the San Juan de Fuca Plate beneath the North American Plate.

▶ WHERE IS THE SAN ANDREAS FAULT?

The San Andreas fault is in western California, near the Pacific coast of the USA. It is named after a lake to the south of the city of San Francisco.

The San Andreas fault and the less famous Fairweather fault in Alaska form the boundary between the Pacific Plate and the North American Plate. The Pacific Plate is slowly rotating anti-clockwise. West of the San Andreas fault, the land is moving north-westwards. The result is that a 2400-kilometre-long stretch of America from north of San Francisco to the tip of Baja California is being slowly moved along the coast at an average rate of 5.3 centimetres a year. But it moves in a series of jumps, causing earthquakes along the fault. San Francisco was badly damaged by an earthquake in 1906 (shown here), when the fault jumped 6.5 metres. The next big jump will probably be near Los Angeles, which lies further south along the fault.

◀ WHERE IS THE GREAT RIFT VALLEY?

The Great Rift Valley is a series of linked rift valleys which stretch for 6500 kilometres from north of the River Jordan, via the Dead Sea and the Red Sea, through Ethiopia and East Africa to the coast near the mouth of the Zambezi River.

A rift valley occurs when a narrow strip of the Earth's crust sinks between roughly parallel faults. The Great Rift Valley is between 30 and 60 kilometres wide and has steep fault scarps on each side for most of its length. The Red Sea fills part of its length. Elsewhere there are long, narrow, deep lakes such as Turkana, Mobutu, Tanganyika and Malawi. In East Africa, the route of the Rift Valley splits into two branches, on either side of Lake Victoria. Faulting probably began about 13 million years ago, and earthquakes and volcanic activity have accompanied the subsequent subsidence and uplift.

▶ WHERE WILL THE CONTINENTS BE IN ANOTHER 50 MILLION YEARS?

The map shows where the continents might be *if* they continue to move at their present rate. The shape of the continents will change, as will their locations.

Around 250 million years ago, ancient continents moved together to form one land mass (Pangea) and one vast ocean (Panthalassa). About 150 million years ago Pangea began to split up, and this process continues today. The Pacific Ocean is all that remains of Panthalassa, and is likely to get smaller. The Americas will be pushed farther west, and will separate as the Atlantic Ocean widens. Australia will be farther north; Eurasia farther south and east.

Smaller pieces of land will move, too. California west of the San Andreas fault will be well on its way to join Alaska. Africa will split, making the Mediterranean smaller.

◀ WHERE ARE THE OLDEST ROCKS?

The oldest piece of rock that has been dated is a piece of gneiss from the Ameralik Fiord in western Greenland. It is about 3800 million years old.

Gneiss is a metamorphic rock – one that has been changed by heat and pressure. It is one of many ancient rocks that form Greenland and the neighbouring Canadian Shield. These rocks are the ancient base of the North American continent. The samples were dated by measuring the rate of change of tiny amounts of radioactive rubidium and strontium in the rock.

It is significant that the oldest rocks have been found on a land area. For it shows how long-lasting the lighter rocks of the continents are. In contrast, the oldest known rocks of the ocean floors are only 200 million years old. It is beneath the oceans that the Earth's crust is being created and destroyed.

▲ WHERE CAN YOU SEE OVER 1500 MILLION YEARS OF ROCK STRATA?

The Colorado Desert in the south-west of the USA has layers of rock which have formed over a period of about 1600 million years. The River Colorado and its tributaries have sliced through these layers in the Grand Canyon and other nearby canyons.

The Grand Canyon area is the only place on Earth where geologists can study so many layers of undisturbed rock and an almost perfect sequence of fossils.

The 'Granite Gorge' at the bottom of the Grand Canyon is cut into the rocks that form the base of most of North America. These ancient rocks were formed about 1700 million years ago. They are buried beneath horizontal layers of rocks. At the bottom of the pile is the Tapeats Sandstone, 570 million years old. At the top of the pile, on the rim of the Canyon, is the Kaibab Limestone, about 270 million years old. Layers of more recent rocks have been eroded from the top of the Grand Canyon.

The rocks of the top of the Grand Canyon form the base of Zion Canyon. This canyon is cut into sandstones that are 150 to 200 million years old. The youngest rocks in Zion Canyon form the base of Bryce Canyon where 60 million-year old shales, sandstones and limestones have been eroded into countless spires. The youngest rocks of the Colorado Plateau are at Brian Head, the plateau's highest point, and are only 37 million years old.

▼ WHERE DO CRYSTALS FORM?

Crystals form either where a solution has evaporated slowly or where molten rock has cooled slowly beneath the surface. The best crystals are those which have the space and the time to form slowly.

You can make salt crystals by leaving seawater (or a strong salt solution) undisturbed to evaporate slowly.

Where a hot mineral solution forces its way into cracks in rocks, and then cools down very slowly, crystals may grow in any spaces left as the solution cools and shrinks. You may find beautiful crystals of quartz or calcite in rocks that have been veined with mineral solutions millions of years ago. Igneous rocks are formed from a variety of molten minerals which cool to form rocks. If the hot rock cools very slowly, the minerals will grow large. Granite is a rock which cooled deep in the Earth's crust. If you look at a granite sample you can see crystals of quartz and feldspar.

▲ WHERE ARE DIAMONDS FOUND?

Diamonds were formed deep underground in conditions of intense heat and pressure. The pictures show an uncut diamond and one that has been cut and polished.

Artificial diamonds can be made in factories. Pure carbon is baked under great pressure to over 1400°C. Natural diamonds probably formed under similar conditions.

Diamonds are thought to have been formed millions of years ago from carbon which was caught up in molten rock deep in the Earth's crust. This molten rock reached the surface in a few places in the form of tube-like 'pipes'. As it cooled, it turned into a rock called kimberlite. Kimberlite pipes are mined for diamonds in South Africa, Tanzania and Siberia. But many diamonds come from the gravels of rivers which once eroded away kimberlite pipes. Such diamonds are found in many parts of Africa, India, Indonesia, Brazil, Australia and the USSR.

▼ WHERE ARE THE BEST PLACES TO LOOK FOR GOLD?

Gold is found in mineral veins in rocks, or in gravels which have been washed away from areas where gold-bearing rocks have been eroded. Prospectors may pan the gravel in streams for grains of gold, as shown in the photograph.

Gold is sometimes found with quartz veins where extremely hot solutions containing molten gold have cooled in cracks and joints in the rocks. Rich veins have been found in areas of recent volcanic activity, earthquakes and mountain-building, such as the mountains on the western edge of the American continents. Famous gold rushes took place in Alaska, California and the Andes, and in 1980 a rich new find was made in the Chilean Andes.

Placer deposits are those washed down with river gravels or moved by ice. Much of South Africa's gold comes from mines reaching down to ancient gravels which formed a rock called conglomerate.

▼ WHERE IS THE WORLD'S GREATEST MOUNTAIN RANGE?

The greatest mountain range on land is the Himalaya-Karakoram Range to the north of India. It has most of the world's highest peaks.

The Andes of South America are a longer but lower mountain range. There are also great mountain ranges beneath the oceans, the longest of which stretches from the Gulf of Aden to the Gulf of California.

'Himalaya' means 'abode of snow' in Sanskrit, an ancient Indian language. This great mountain range stretches about 2500 kilometres from east to west and 80 to 150 kilometres from north to south. Seventy-nine peaks are over 7500 metres high.

The Himalayas were formed in the last 35 million years at the boundary of two crustal plates, the Indian Plate and the Eurasian Plate. When the edges of these two crustal plates collided, they crumpled to form a great mountain range.

▼ WHERE IS THE LARGEST ACTIVE VOLCANO?

The highest active volcanoes on land are in the Andes, in South America. But even larger volcanoes rise from the floor of the Pacific Ocean and form the islands of Hawaii.

Mauna Loa, on Hawaii, is probably the largest active volcano in the world. It rises 4170 metres above sea level, but its base is 5180 metres below sea level. This base is roughly oval in shape: 119 kilometres long and 85 kilometres across. So a colossal amount of volcanic material forms this mountain.

The lava from Hawaiian volcanoes (shown here) is very liquid and flows for long distances. Mauna Loa erupts about every 3½ years. Kilauea Crater, south-east of the main volcano, is filled with a red-hot lava lake called Halemaumau, 'The Fire Pit'.

Volcanoes in the Andes reach higher above sea level than Mauna Loa. Ojos del Salada, on the border of Argentina and Chile, is 6885 metres high.

▲ WHERE IS THE WORLD'S HIGHEST MOUNTAIN?

Mount Everest is the highest mountain on land: 8848 metres high. It is in the Himalayas, on the border of Nepal and Tibet.

The height of Mount Everest was discovered in 1852. It was named after Sir George Everest, the Surveyor-General of India at the time. It is called *Sagarmatha* in Nepalese and *Miti Guti Chapu Long-na* in Tibetan.

Like the other high peaks of the Himalayas, Everest is snow-covered all year. Avalanches are common and glaciers fill the valleys. These present great difficulties to climbers, who also face low temperatures, high winds and lack of oxygen.

Although the top of Everest is the highest point of the Earth's surface, it is not the tallest mountain when measured from base to peak. Mauna Kea on Hawaii is a total of 10,023 metres tall – only 4205 metres above sea level but its base is 5818 metres below the Pacific.

WHERE HAS A VOLCANO GIVEN BIRTH TO AN ISLAND?

The photograph shows Surtsey, an island off the coast of Iceland that was born in a flurry of steam and boiling sea in November 1963. It is just one of many thousands of islands that are volcanoes. Vulcano, an Italian island rising from the Mediterranean Sea, gave its name to all volcanoes.

The mid-Atlantic Ridge is a string of volcanoes down the middle of the Atlantic Ocean. These volcanoes often erupt as new material is added to the Earth's crust. The ridge rises above sea level in Iceland, where there are many active volcanoes, lava flows, geysers and hot springs. Tristan da Cunha is another volcano on the same ridge, but far away in the South Atlantic.

The Pacific has many island volcanoes. An arc-shaped pattern of volcanic islands is found near many of the deep-sea trenches, such as the Aleutian Islands. Other volcanoes rise from the ocean floor above 'hot spots' beneath the Earth's crust. Examples include the Hawaiian Islands in the Pacific and the Azores in the Atlantic.

WHERE WAS THE BIGGEST VOLCANIC ERUPTION?

The biggest explosion in history happened in 1883 when the island of Krakatoa, in Indonesia, was blown to bits. In 1815, another Indonesian volcano, Tambora, produced the most matter discharged in any known eruption.

Krakatoa was an island in the Sunda Straits between Sumatra and Java. Before 1883 it covered 47 square kilometres. The eruption of 27 August 1883 woke people in Australia and India, 3000 kilometres away. Rocks were hurled 55 kilometres up into the atmosphere and volcanic dust fell on places over 5000 kilometres away. Tidal waves caused as much damage and more deaths than the eruption itself. For three years after Krakatoa exploded, the fine dust in the upper atmosphere cooled the weather and caused amazing sunsets in Europe.

Today, a small volcano is growing in the remains of the old volcano.

▼ WHICH VOLCANO
DESTROYED AN ANCIENT
ROMAN TOWN?

Mount Vesuvius rises above the Bay of Naples in southern Italy. In AD 79 this volcano erupted and buried Pompeii, Herculaneum and other Roman towns.

Mount Vesuvius had been dormant for 800 years. Few people realized that it was a volcano, and those who did thought it was extinct. Fine towns were built on the Bay of Naples, and the rich soil on the slopes of Vesuvius was farmed. Then, on 24 August 79 AD Mount Vesuvius suddenly erupted. Gases trapped inside built up such pressure that tonnes of lava, pumice and ash were blown out.

For three days Pompeii was bombarded with pumice and ash. About 16,000 people died. But the ash preserved minute details of Roman life for archaeologists.

Nearby Herculaneum was buried under 13 metres of boiling mud. Vesuvius was blown apart in the eruption. But part of the wall of the old crater still exists.

▼ WHERE IS THE PACIFIC
'RING OF FIRE'?

When the world's volcanoes are plotted on a map, the Pacific Ocean appears surrounded by a ring of fiery volcanic activity.

Around the Pacific Ocean there are many active volcanoes. Some of the world's highest volcanoes are in the Andes and the mountains of Central America. Other volcanoes are found in the mountains of the western USA and Alaska. The Aleutians are a chain of volcanic islands. There are more active volcanoes in the Kamchatka Peninsula of the USSR, and in Japan, Papua-New Guinea and New Zealand. In addition, huge volcanoes rise from the Pacific Ocean floor to form Hawaii and other islands.

Most of the volcanoes that ring the Pacific are found quite near the deep sea trenches at the edge of the ocean. They are caused by the destruction of the Pacific Ocean Plate as it disappears beneath the surrounding continental plates.

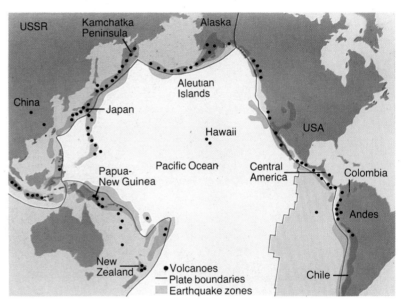

▲ WHERE HAVE THE
STRONGEST EARTHQUAKES
OCCURRED?

The strongest earthquakes so far this century have occurred in Colombia (in 1906); San Francisco, USA (1906); China (1920 and 1976); Japan (1923); Assam, India (1950); Kamchatka, USSR (1952); Aleutians (1957); Chile (1960); Alaska (1964).

Earthquakes are usually measured on a scale devised by Charles Richter in 1954. Since 1977, the biggest quakes have been recorded on the Kanamori scale. On this new scale, the strongest earthquake this century occurred at Lebu, in Chile on 22 May 1960. It measured 9.5 on the Kanamori scale. A 300-kilometre long stretch of the coast sank two metres into the Pacific. Shock waves were felt round the Earth for two weeks.

Many serious earthquakes have occurred around the Pacific Ocean. Like volcanoes, they are caused by movement at the edges of crustal plates.

▶ WHERE DOES MUD BOIL?

Boiling mud is one of the side-effects of volcanic activity. Hot water and gases from beneath the surface bubble through the mud, so that it looks like a pan of boiling porridge!

Boiling mud is found in a number of volcanic areas of the world. Volcanic gases such as sulphur, which create the heat and boiling effect, usually give the mud an evil smell. But the associated minerals are thought to promote healing, so

mud pools are often health centres.

People visit the Italian island of Vulcano to be coated in hot, smelly mud as a cure for rheumatism. Similar healing centres thrive near the hot mud pools and springs of the volcanic plateau in North Island, New Zealand.

Boiling mud is still found where volcanoes have been inactive for centuries, such as on the West Indian island of St Lucia. This shows that heat is still coming from deep down, and volcanic activity is not dead.

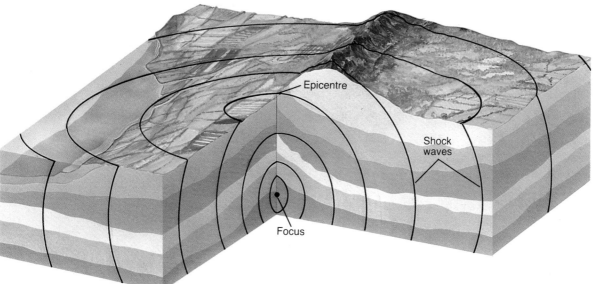

Epicentre

Shock waves

Focus

▲ WHERE IS THE EPICENTRE OF AN EARTHQUAKE?

The epicentre of an earthquake is the point on the Earth's surface immediately above the place where the movement of the Earth's crust has caused shock waves.

Earthquakes occur where rock layers are moving against one another on a fault line. Sudden release of the tension sends out shock waves (called seismic waves) in all directions. The point from which the seismic

waves radiate is called the focus. As the diagram shows, the epicentre is at the Earth's surface above the focus.

The depth of an earthquake is the distance between the focus and the epicentre. Seismologists (people who study earthquakes) classify earthquakes as shallow if the focus is less than 50 kilometres beneath the epicentre, and deep if the focus is more than 200 kilometres below.

As the epicentre is the closest point to the focus, it feels the shocks first and usually suffers the most

damage. Surface waves radiate out from the epicentre and damage surrounding areas.

Deep earthquakes are felt over great distances. The 1897 earthquake in Assam, northern India, was one of the deepest on record. Tremors were felt in Rome, Strasbourg and Edinburgh.

Shallow earthquakes may cause great damage near the epicentre but are less noticeable farther away. The 1960 earthquake at Agadir, Morocco, flattened the city centre, yet a kilometre away there was little damage.

▲ WHERE ARE THE WORLD'S HOTTEST PLACES?

The highest shade temperature on record is 58°C in September 1922 at Al'Aziziyah in the Sahara Desert in Libya. Nearly as hot was the 56.7°C recorded in Death Valley in the USA, in July 1913.

You might expect the hottest places to be on the Equator. Although equatorial lands are hot all year, they are also very cloudy. The hot deserts are near the Tropics where the sun is overhead in mid-summer. Because there is very little rain, there is very little cloud, so it is sunny and hot all day.

The eastern Sahara has more sunshine than anywhere else: sunshine has been recorded for 4300 hours in a year. That is an average of 11 hours 47 minutes per day. So it is not surprising that the highest temperature on record occurred in the Sahara.

The picture shows Death Valley, where temperatures up to 50°C in summer are not unusual. This is also a desert area.

▲ WHERE ARE THE WORLD'S COLDEST PLACES?

The coldest temperatures are recorded in winter in Antarctica. In July 1983, Russian scientists measured a new record low of −89.2°C.

Until modern weather stations were set up in Antarctica, the coldest temperatures were recorded in Siberia: −68°C was recorded at Verkhoyansk in 1892. Verkhoyansk holds the record for experiencing the greatest temperature range: from a coldest winter temperature of −68°C to a hottest summer temperature of 36.7°C.

The Arctic 'cold pole' is some way from the North Pole because of the surrounding Arctic Ocean. Seas have a moderating effect on the climate of coastal areas. Verkhoyansk is inland from the Arctic Ocean, and a long way from any other sea. The huge land-mass of Eurasia heats up quickly in summer to give surprisingly high temperatures even in the far north, but it loses its heat quickly in winter.

▲ WHERE DOES FROST COME FROM?

Frost is small crystals of ice which cling to any surface such as twigs, blades of grass or windows. It forms when the temperature is low enough for water vapour in the air to condense as ice instead of as water droplets.

The air around us always contains some water vapour. Cold air can hold less water vapour than warm air. At the end of a warm day the air will cool down. If the air is moist and still, some of the water vapour will condense as mist or dew. If the temperature falls below freezing, ice crystals will form instead of water droplets. A coating of ice crystals is called frost.

Frost is especially likely on a clear calm night. If there is no cloud cover to act as a blanket over the surface of the Earth, heat will radiate back into the atmosphere very quickly, and temperatures will fall fast. Because cold air tends to sink, frost may occur in hollows and valley bottoms and not on the hill slopes above.

▲ WHERE ARE THE
WETTEST PLACES ON
EARTH?

Cherrapunji, in India, holds the record for the most rain in one month: 9299 millimetres in July 1861. It also had the most rain in a year: 26,461 millimetres in the year up to 31 July 1861. Mount Wai-'ale-'ale in Hawaii has the most rainy days (350 a year), and the highest average annual rainfall.

Very high rainfall occurs when warm, moist winds are forced to rise. As the air cools, the water vapour condenses as rain.

Cherrapunji clings to a hillside in Assam, in north-east India. It faces the full force of the monsoon winds as they sweep north from the Indian Ocean in July. As the warm, wet winds rise towards the Himalayas, torrential rain falls for a few weeks. The photograph shows dense rain-forest in Assam.

The Hawaiian mountains are wet all year. They are in the path of the North-East Trade Winds which pick up moisture from the vast Pacific Ocean. This causes the record rainfall on Mount Wai-'ale-'ale. It has 350 rainy days a year, and has the highest average annual rainfall: 11,455 millimetres.

▲ WHERE IS THE DRIEST
PLACE ON EARTH?

The photograph shows the Atacama Desert in northern Chile, where the first rain for 400 years fell in 1971. All deserts are dry, but the Atacama is the driest.

The Atacama Desert is hemmed in between the Pacific Ocean and the Andes mountains. The Andes shut out all winds from the east. Like the other hot deserts of the world, the Atacama lies astride one of the Tropics where air pressure is high. The air descends and is therefore warm and dry. There is little cloud, so the sunny days are intensely hot but the starry nights can be cold.

The Atacama Desert is exceptionally dry, but rainfall is very low in all desert areas. Cairo, in the eastern Sahara, averages 28 millimetres a year. Bahrain, on the edge of the Arabian Desert has 81 millimetres. But average rainfall figures for deserts can be confusing: there may be heavy storms on a few days in some years, and almost continuous drought in others.

Not all the dry parts of the Earth are also hot. Large areas of Central Asia are sheltered by mountains from any rain-bearing winds. Yet deserts such as the Gobi are very cold in winter. The Polar lands are also very dry – although the moisture that does fall accumulates as snow.

WHERE ARE THE WORLD'S LONGEST GLACIERS?

Eight of the world's ten longest glaciers are in Antarctica. The longest is the Lambert-Fisher Ice Passage, which has a total length of 515 kilometres.

Petermanns Glacier in Greenland is the largest glacier in the northern hemisphere, and extends 40 kilometres out to sea.

The largest glaciers are fed with ice from the great ice sheets covering Antarctica and Greenland. Greenland has the fastest-moving glacier: the Quarayaq advances at 20-24 metres a day.

Spectacular glaciers are found elsewhere in the world. The longest Himalayan glacier is the Siachen (76 kilometres long) in the Karakoram Range. Also in the Himalayas, the Hispar and Biafo Glaciers join to form an ice passage 122 kilometres long.

Among the world's twenty longest glaciers are those in North America (in Alaska), Asia (in the Pamirs), in New Zealand and in the Alps.

WHERE ARE THE WORLD'S BIGGEST EXPANSES OF ICE?

Just over 10 per cent of the land surface of the world is permanently covered by ice. Most of the world's ice (87 per cent) is in Antarctica. The Arctic has 12.5 per cent (mainly covering Greenland), and the rest is found in the glaciers which exist on every continent.

Antarctica is covered almost completely by the world's

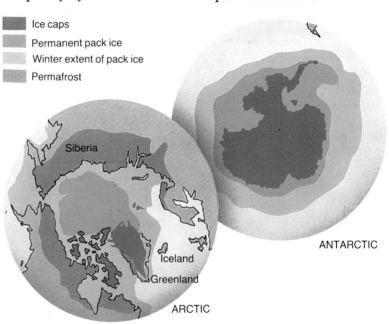

Ice caps
Permanent pack ice
Winter extent of pack ice
Permafrost

Siberia

Iceland

Greenland

ARCTIC

ANTARCTIC

largest ice sheet and only a few edges of the shore are exposed. In all, there are 13,600,000 square kilometres of ice. The thickest ice recorded was 4776 metres in depth.

The North Pole is an ocean area, and the largest area of land ice is on Greenland where the ice sheet covers 1,700,000 square kilometres. It is about 3000 metres thick at its centre.

The total amount of ice outside the Polar regions is very small. The largest expanse is in Iceland: 8800 square kilometres.

▲ WHERE IS PERMAFROST FOUND?

Permafrost is permanently frozen ground. It is found beneath permanent ice and snow. It is also found in large areas around the Arctic Ocean where the snow melts in summer but only the top few centimetres of the soil thaw.

Permafrost covers the whole of Antarctica. In the Arctic, permafrost is shallowest near the coast and deepest inland where the weather is coldest.

Permafrost 1370 metres deep has been found in Siberia.

In summer, when the snow melts and the topsoil thaws, water cannot drain into the frozen ground below. The whole surface is marshy.

It is difficult to build on permafrost. Heated buildings have to be insulated from the ground beneath, else they defrost the soil and sink into the mud. Permafrost is also a great hindrance to oil-drilling and mining. But it has preserved the remains of ancient animals, such as woolly mammoths.

▼ WHERE ARE THE BIGGEST ICEBERGS FOUND?

The icebergs with the biggest area are the tabular icebergs that break away from Antarctica. The largest ever seen was over 31,000 square kilometres (bigger than Belgium). The tallest icebergs break away from Greenland. The tallest ever seen was 167 metres above the water.

The iceberg with the largest area was seen in the South Pacific in 1956. The huge icebergs in this area have broken away from the Ross Ice Shelf. There, the Antarctic ice sheet extends out over the sea in an ice shelf as large as France. Its ice cliffs tower up to 50 metres above the sea. Along its 650 kilometre front it cracks with the rise and fall of the tide. Enormous icebergs break loose and float northwards into the Pacific.

The very tall Arctic icebergs are especially dangerous as eight-ninths of the ice is hidden beneath the sea.

ARCTIC ICEBERGS

TABULAR ICEBERGS

▲ WHERE DO ICEBERGS MELT?

Icebergs gradually melt as they float away from the Polar lands. But how long it takes will depend on the size of the iceberg and the temperature of the sea.

Melting icebergs have been seen very close to tropical waters. In 1935, an Arctic iceberg was recorded at latitude 28½°N in the North Atlantic. And in 1894 a ship recorded an iceberg in the Atlantic at latitude 26½°S.

As icebergs drift away from the Polar regions they are melted by the sun and by warmer water. Waves and rain erode them further. An iceberg may actually break apart while drifting, and if this disturbs its balance it may roll over. As an iceberg melts, the rocks in the ice sink to the sea bed.

Cold ocean currents carry icebergs far away from their point of origin. When the cold Labrador Current continues further south than usual, it brings Arctic icebergs into the busy North Atlantic shipping route.

▼ WHERE ARE CREVASSES FOUND?

Crevasses are cracks in the ice of glaciers and ice sheets. They are often quite narrow, but extremely deep and dangerous, especially if hidden by a thin crust of frozen snow.

The great mass of ice in a glacier or ice sheet moves slowly downhill. But the surface layers are always rigid and brittle. Different parts of a glacier move at different rates: the surface moves faster than the base, and the centre of the surface moves faster than the sides.

The different rates of flow create tensions in the ice and cause cracks in the surface layers. Whenever a glacier flows round a bend or over a hump, or changes its speed for some other reason, crevasses and pressure ridges form.

At the head of a mountain glacier there is an especially deep crevasse called the Bergschrund. This forms where the glacier ice is pulling away from the permanent snow on the mountain slope.

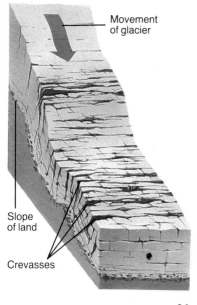

Movement of glacier

Slope of land

Crevasses

▼ WHERE IS THE GREATEST OCEAN CURRENT?

The greatest ocean current is the West Wind Drift (also called the Antarctic Circumpolar Current). Its cold waters originate near the Antarctic and encircle that continent. The current is driven along by strong Westerly Winds.

The West Wind Drift varies in width from 200 to 300 kilometres. Its surface flow is less than one kilometre an hour. Measurements made in Drake Passage, where the current is squeezed between South America and Antarctica, recorded a flow of water at 270 million cubic metres per second – three times the greatest flow of the Gulf Stream.

The West Wind Drift is driven along by the strong Westerly Winds of the southern hemisphere. These are called the Roaring Forties because they blow at latitudes 40°-50°S. There are few land obstacles this far south to either wind or ocean current. Here there are some of the roughest seas and fiercest gales.

▼ WHERE ARE THE DOLDRUMS?

The Doldrums is a name given by early sailors to a zone at the Equator where winds are often light, their direction uncertain and where sailing ships were often becalmed.

For sailors in sailing ships, the Doldrums were a great contrast to the Trade Winds which blow steadily in the zone between the Tropics and the Equator. The North-East and South-East Trade Winds converge on the Equator where pressure is low and the air rises.

Because the air rises at the Equator there is plenty of rain. Sudden squalls and thunderstorms occur frequently, even though, in general, winds blow along the surface lightly. Sailing in such conditions is difficult because the boat is not carried along in any particular direction.

The exact location of the Doldrums moves with the seasons. In June they are about 5° north of the Equator, and in December they are about 5° south.

▼ WHERE IS THE GULF STREAM?

The Gulf Stream is a warm ocean current which begins in the Gulf of Mexico and flows across the North Atlantic towards Europe.

The Gulf Stream bursts into the Atlantic through the Straits of Florida, between the USA and Cuba. It flows close to the coast of America as far as Cape Hatteras and then continues north-east towards Europe. In the open ocean it is driven along by the Westerly Winds.

The Gulf Stream is a meandering current about 100 kilometres wide. Its average speed is less than one kilometre an hour. To the north of the Gulf Stream there is a very sudden change to cold water. And as it is only a surface current, the water temperature cools rapidly below 350 metres.

The warm water of the Gulf Stream is vital to northern Europe. Ports are ice-free and the weather is warm enough for farming much further north in Europe than in eastern Canada on the opposite side of the Atlantic.

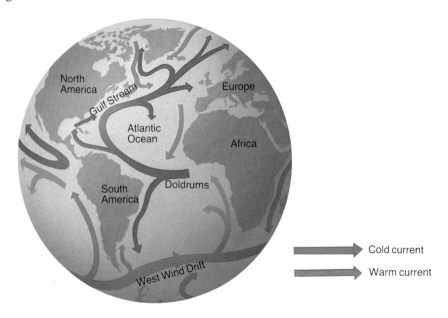

▶ WHERE IS THE ABYSSAL PLAIN?

'Abyss' usually means the lowest depth of the oceans. The abyssal plain is the deep ocean floor. As the diagram shows, it lies nearly 4000 metres beneath the ocean surface. Large areas are almost flat and featureless. The abyssal plain has been called 'the smoothest surface on Earth'. But in places the plain is broken up by deep chasms and sea mountains.

The abyssal plain covers about two-thirds of the ocean floor. It begins at the foot of the steep continental slope. Here, sediments have slumped off the slope and been dumped by muddy currents. Away from the continental slope, the layer of sediments on the abyssal plain thins out and its slope becomes almost level.

Features such as under-sea volcanoes and deep ocean trenches break up the flat surface of the abyssal plain. These occur at the margins of crustal plates. There are also isolated sea-mounts, only a few of which reach the surface to form islands.

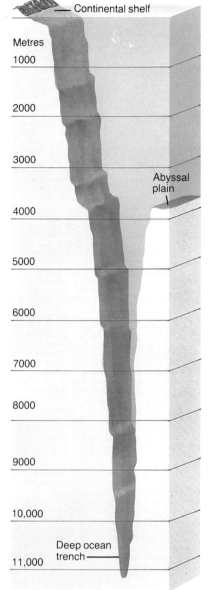

Continental shelf

Metres
1000

2000

3000

Abyssal plain

4000

5000

6000

7000

8000

9000

10,000

Deep ocean trench

11,000

◀ WHERE IS THE DEEPEST PART OF THE OCEAN?

The deepest part of the ocean was found in 1951 by the survey ship *Challenger*. Echo-soundings showed that part of the Mariana Trench, south of Japan, is 10,900 metres deep. In 1960 the US Navy bathyscaphe *Trieste* descended to the bottom of the Challenger Deep.

The Mariana Trench is one of many deep-sea trenches around the edges of the Pacific Ocean. These V-shaped trenches are parallel to a continent or line of islands.

A deep-sea trench plunges down from the abyssal plain. It may be 50-100 kilometres wide at the top, but only a few kilometres wide at the bottom. Most are found in the Pacific, but they also occur in the Caribbean, the South Atlantic and the Indian Ocean.

Deep-sea trenches mark places where the ocean floor is being subducted beneath a continental plate. Scientists are studying sediments in the deep trenches, which might one day be used for dumping dangerous waste materials.

◀ WHICH SEA IS THE SALTIEST?

The Dead Sea, on the borders of Israel and Jordan, is the world's saltiest sea. It is over ten times saltier than the average ocean.

The Dead Sea has no exit. Most of its water comes from the north, in the River Jordan. Mineral springs at the bottom of the Dead Sea, and around its shores, add to the salts in the water. The climate is very hot and dry, so an enormous amount of water is lost by evaporation. Salts in the water are therefore very concentrated. They are extracted in large evaporation pans. The picture shows natural salt deposits in the Dead Sea.

The shores of the Dead Sea are the lowest exposed point on the Earth's surface: 393 metres below sea level.

To the south is the Red Sea, the saltiest part of the open sea. Here, too, the salt is concentrated because so much water evaporates in the hot sun and so little is added from the surrounding desert.

▼ WHERE IS THE LARGEST ARCHIPELAGO?

An archipelago is a sea studded with islands. The word was first used for the Aegean Sea with its many Greek islands. The largest archipelago is in South-East Asia where thousands of islands make up the countries of Indonesia, eastern Malaysia and the Philippines.

The country of Indonesia is made up of over 13,000 islands of which about 3000 are inhabited. The islands stretch over 5000 kilometres from west of the Malay Peninsula to New Guinea. Many of the islands in Indonesia are volcanoes. They form a great arc to the north of a deep-sea trench called the Java Trench.

Indonesia shares two of its islands with two other countries. Eastern Malaysia is part of the island of Borneo, and Papua-New Guinea shares an island with West Irian.

There are over 7000 islands in the Philippines, although more than 90 per cent of the land area consists of just the eleven largest islands.

▼ WHERE DO TIDAL BORES OCCUR?

A tidal bore is a high wave which travels up an estuary as the tide comes in. Such bores are only found where there is a big tidal range and a funnel-shaped estuary.

As the tide rises in a river estuary, it is held back by the shallow water and the out-flowing river current. This causes the water to pile up and move up the river like a large breaking wave.

The most remarkable bore is on the River Ch'ient'ang'kian which flows into the Bay of Hangchow (Hangzhou) in China. Each spring tide, the bore is 7.5 metres high, and travels at 24 kilometres an hour. It can be heard coming 22 kilometres away!

The tidal bore with the greatest volume flows up the Canal do Norte, the main exit of the River Amazon. One of the fastest tidal bores flows up the River Hooghly, which is a branch of the River Ganges.

In contrast the tidal bore on the River Severn in England is only just over a metre high.

▲ WHERE ARE THE WORLD'S HIGHEST TIDES?

The greatest rise and fall of the tide is recorded in the Bay of Fundy, between New Brunswick and Nova Scotia provinces in eastern Canada. The average spring tide range is 14.5 metres, though tidal ranges of up to 16.3 metres are recorded.

The tides of the Atlantic Ocean are funnelled into the narrow Bay of Fundy to produce the largest tidal range. This enormous range creates a tidal bore in the bay, even though it is not the estuary of a major river. The tidal flow enriches the marine life in the water, and the Bay is a haven for wading birds.

In Europe, the Rance estuary in northern France has a large tidal range. It is the site of the world's first tidal power station.

Unexpected high tides can cause great damage. They are usually the result of tidal surges, caused by very high winds and low air pressure at the same time as the expected high tide.

▼ WHERE IS THE LONGEST REEF IN THE WORLD?

The Great Barrier Reef, off the north-east coast of Australia, is the world's longest coral reef. It stretches for over 2000 kilometres from near Papua to the centre of the Queensland coast.

Coral reefs can only form in tropical seas where the water is warm and shallow enough for the coral polyps to flourish. Like many other reefs, the Great Barrier Reef plunges into water which is too deep for corals to survive today. But sea level was probably much lower in the past when the reef first began to form.

The Great Barrier Reef lies between 45 and 65 kilometres off the Australian coast. In the north it is only 15-20 kilometres wide, but in the south the reef area extends up to 325 kilometres out to sea. There are only about ten safe passages through the reef, so it is a perilous area to navigate.

More than 340 varieties of coral have been identified on the reef. They present an incredible array of colours and shapes and are the homes of many beautiful fish and other sea creatures. Recently, parts of the reef have been destroyed by the Crown of Thorns starfish which sucks the living polyps off the hard coral skeletons.

▼ WHERE ARE FIORDS FOUND?

Fiords are long, narrow, steep-sided inlets of the sea. They were made by glaciers which deepened the valleys along which they flowed. After the glaciers disappeared, their U-shaped valleys were flooded by the sea to form fiords.

Fiords are found on mountainous coasts which have been eroded by glaciers. The fiords of Norway are famous and are among the longest in the world. Sogne Fiord is 183 kilometres long from the open sea to the head of Lusterfiord. Its average width is 4.75 kilometres. Like most fiords, it is exceptionally deep, but becomes shallower towards the coast. At its deepest point, Sogne Fiord is 1245 metres deep.

Even longer is the Nordvest Fiord arm of Scoresby Sound in eastern Greenland. This fiord is 313 kilometres long.

Fiords are also found along the coast of Iceland, the Pacific coast of Canada and Alaska, in southern Chile and in South Island, New Zealand. The picture shows a village at the head of a Norwegian fjord.

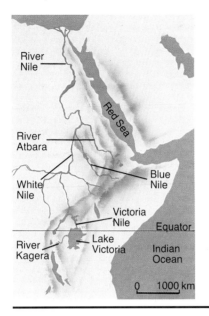

◄ WHICH IS THE LONGEST RIVER?

The three longest rivers in the world are the Nile in Africa: 6670 kilometres long; the Amazon in South America: 6448 kilometres; and the Mississippi-Missouri in North America: 5970 kilometres.

Different experts give different lengths for these great rivers. This is because it is not easy to say exactly where a river begins and where it ends. All have many tributaries, and there are many channels in their deltas.

Does the Nile begin in Lake Victoria, as some books say? The furthest source of the Nile is the Luvironzo in Burundi, which flows into the Kagera and then into Lake Victoria.

The furthest source of the Amazon was discovered in Peru in 1953. But where does the river end? The Canal do Norte is usually classed as the main exit. But the Rio Para is also navigable, and if this counts as an exit, then the Amazon is 6750 kilometres long.

► WHICH IS THE LARGEST RIVER?

The River Amazon is larger than the River Nile. The Amazon drains nearly twice as big an area. It contains far more water, and boats can travel much farther upstream.

The two major tributaries of the Nile, the White Nile and the Blue Nile, begin in areas with quite high rainfall. But for most of its course the Nile flows through desert where little water is added and a lot of water evaporates. Consequently, the flow of the Nile is very low for a major river: an average discharge of 3120 cubic metres per second. All the world's major rivers, except the Murray-Darling in Australia, have a greater flow.

The River Amazon carries a greater volume of water than any other river: its average discharge is 180,000 cubic metres per second. Its many long tributaries drain an area of over seven million square kilometres, most of which receives heavy rain all year through.

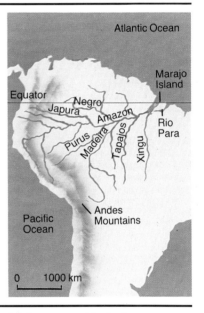

◄ WHERE ARE THE HIGHEST WATERFALLS?

The highest falls in the world are the Angel Falls on the Carrao River, a tributary of the Caroni River, in Venezuela, South America. The total fall of water is 979 metres; the longest single drop is 807 metres.

The Angel Falls are one of several very high waterfalls in this part of Venezuela, most of which are unmeasured and unnamed. They occur where rivers flow over the edge of a high, steep-sided plateau.

The Angel Falls have long been known to the local Indians who call them Cherun-Meru. Europeans first saw them in 1910. They were then re-discovered in 1937 by an American pilot named Jimmy Angel who crash-landed nearby.

The world's second highest falls are the Tugela Falls in Natal, South Africa. The Tugela River drops 947 metres at the falls. In Norway, the Utigard Falls carry water from the melting Jostedal Glacier 800 metres into Nesdal.

▶ WHERE WERE THE WORST FLOODS RECORDED?

Some of the world's worst floods have occurred when the Hwang-ho River in China has burst its banks. Floods in 1931 killed over 3,500,000 people.

Hwang-ho means 'Yellow River' and it is the muddiest river in the world. It flows for 4800 kilometres through northern China and carries over 1500 million tonnes of silt. About a quarter of this silt is dumped near the mouth of the river, to raise the river bed and alter the course of the river channel. For thousands of years dykes have been built to prevent flooding but when the dykes burst disaster occurs.

The main flood season is from July to September, when most of the rain falls. But there are problems in spring-time too, when the southern part of the river thaws while the great loop to the north is still iced up. Sluice gates on the Hwang-ho, like those shown in the picture, are now used for flood-control and irrigation.

◀ WHERE IS THE LARGEST LAKE?

The world's largest lake is the Caspian Sea, between Iran and the USSR. Although it is called a sea, it is not connected with the oceans, but is a very large inland lake. Its total area is 371,800 square kilometres.

The surface of the Caspian Sea is 28 metres below sea level, and the deepest point of the lake is a further 980 metres down.

The Volga and Ural rivers both flow into the Caspian. No river flows out. The lake is in a desert area, so a lot of water evaporates and the water is very salty. As more river water is used for irrigation and industry, so less water reaches the Caspian. The world's largest lake is getting smaller.

The largest fresh-water lake is Lake Superior, between the USA and Canada. It covers 82,350 square kilometres. Lake Superior does have an exit: into Lake Huron and the other Great Lakes and then to the Atlantic via the St Lawrence River.

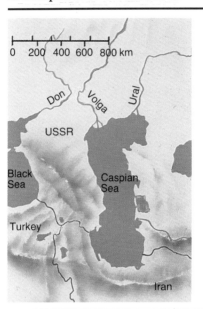

▶ WHERE IS THE HIGHEST LAKE?

The highest lake in the world is an unnamed glacial lake near Mount Everest which lies at 5880 metres above sea level. Tibet's largest lake, Nam Tso is 4578 metres above sea level. The world's highest navigable lake is Lake Titicaca (shown here), on the border of Peru and Bolivia. It is 3811 metres above sea level and is navigated by lake steamers.

The total area of Lake Titicaca is about 8300 square kilometres, and its maximum depth is 370 metres. The lake receives water from several mountain rivers of the Andes. Its water drains south to Lake Poopo, and then disappears into the dry *altiplano* (high plain).

The land around Lake Titicaca is bleak and treeless. Llamas and vicunas graze on the coarse grass. Totoro reeds grow in the lake and are used by the local Indians to make reed fishing-boats, houses and even the islands on which they live.

▲ WHERE IS THE BIGGEST CAVE?

The largest single cavern in the world is the Sarawak Chamber, in Sarawak, Eastern Malaysia. It was discovered in 1980.

The largest cave system in the world is under the Mammoth Cave National Park in the US state of Kentucky.

Sarawak is part of Eastern Malaysia and is on the island of Borneo in South-East Asia. The Sarawak Chamber is under the Gunung Mulu National Park. It was surveyed in 1980 and found to be 700 metres long, an average of 300 metres wide, and at least 70 metres high.

At Mammoth Cave National Park (see photograph), there is a maze of caves and passageways at different levels. The Mammoth Cave system itself is 307.5 kilometres long. Only four kilometres from the entrance to Mammoth Caves is the entrance to Flint Ridge Caves. In 1972, Mrs P. Crowther found an underground route linking the two systems.

▲ WHERE IS THE DEEPEST CAVE?

The deepest cave found so far is the Gouffre Jean Bernard Cave in the French Alps. In 1982, a team of French cavers reached 1494 metres below the surface.

On a five-day expedition in 1982, the Groupe Speleo Vulcain set a new world depth record for cavers. Their route down included a dive through a sump 40 metres long which led them into a new series of descending passages. The final cave was measured as 1494 metres deep.

France has other very deep caves. The Gouffre Berger Caves near Grenoble are 1.1 kilometres deep. Gouffre de la Pierre Saint-Martin in the Pyrenees is now known to be 1350 metres deep.

Snezhnaya Cave in the USSR is now claimed to be the second deepest cave. Explorers have reached 1350 metres down. They could feel a current of air coming through the rubble at the bottom, and hope to find another passage descending even further.

▲ WHERE ARE THE LARGEST STALACTITES AND STALAGMITES?

Stalactites hang down from cave roofs. The largest is in Spain. Stalagmites grow up from cave floors. The largest is in France.

Stalactites and stalagmites grow in caves where water saturated with calcium carbonate drips from the cave roof. The deposits build up very slowly, so large formations have probably been undisturbed for thousands of years.

The largest stalactite is a wall-supported column which hangs down 59 metres from the roof of the Cueva de Nerja, east of Malaga in Spain. The huge cave was discovered in 1959 by a shepherd boy looking for his ball. It is now an underground auditorium for concerts and ballets.

The longest free-hanging stalactite hangs down seven metres in the *Poll an Ionain* cave in County Clare, Ireland.

La Grande Stalagmite in Aven Armand cave in France is the world's tallest. It stands 29 metres high.

► WHERE ARE THE LARGEST SAND DUNES?

The highest measured sand dunes are found in central Algeria, in the Sahara Desert. They stand up to 430 metres high.

Only about a tenth of the Sahara Desert is covered with wind-blown sand. The rest is gravel plains, plateaus and mountains. Most of the sand is found in 25 large sand-seas, called ergs. These are quite distinct from the surrounding sand-free desert.

The highest dunes are found in the sand-sea of Isaouane-n-Tifernine to the north of the Hoggar mountains. The Sahara's largest area of sand dunes is the Grand Erg Oriental, on the border of Algeria and Tunisia. This sand-sea covers about 518,000 square kilometres.

The world's largest area of sand dunes is Rub'-al-Khali, 'the Empty Quarter', in the Arabian Desert. It covers about 650,000 square kilometres of southern Saudi Arabia. The central sand mountains rise to 250 metres.

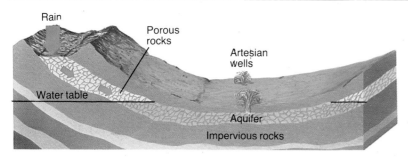

▲ WHERE IS ARTESIAN WATER FOUND?

Artesian water is underground water which rises to the surface under natural pressure. The name comes from Artois in France, **where many wells have been dug to reach artesian water in the underlying chalk.**

The diagram shows how an artesian basin can form. Rain falling on the higher land can flow through the layers of porous rocks. Beneath the low land, the porous rocks are sandwiched between impervious layers. The water-bearing layer is called an aquifer.

In the lowland, a well dug through the top impervious layer will reach the aquifer below. Because the water table (the top of the underground water) is higher than the top of the well, the water will gush to the surface under its own pressure.

The Great Artesian Basin of Australia is the world's largest.

◄ WHERE ARE DESERTS BEING CREATED?

On the edges of some of the Earth's natural deserts, the environment is being upset by poor farming methods and mismanagement.

Semi-desert areas have fragile soils and difficult climates. Several good years are often followed by several bad years. In the good years, farmers may extend the cultivated areas, or increase their flocks and herds, and dig more wells. But in a series of dry years crops fail, animals exhaust the pasture, the bare soil is eroded, and many wells dry up. Such problems created the 'dust bowl' in the USA in the 1930s, and extended the Sahara in the 1970s.

The problem of finding enough fuel for cooking has denuded large areas of semi-desert of all trees and bushes. This makes the soil more prone to erosion. Some areas have been transformed by large irrigation schemes, but poor water management can harm the soil. Then, large areas may revert to desert.

31

▶ WHERE HAS LAND RECLAMATION DOUBLED THE SIZE OF A COUNTRY?

The Netherlands is one of the smallest countries in Europe. Yet half its land area is the result of reclaiming land from marshes, lakes and sea.

The Netherlands lies in the delta area formed by the Rivers Rhine, Meuse (Maas) and Scheldt. Most of the land is below 30 metres, and half the total area below high tide level.

The areas of reclaimed land are called polders. They are surrounded by dykes (banks) to keep out flood-water, and criss-crossed by drainage ditches. The water was once removed by wind pumps, but diesel pumps are used now.

Major modern reclamation schemes include the Zuider Zee and Delta Projects. The Zuider Zee was closed off from the North Sea by a 32-kilometre-long dam in 1932. The former bay was transformed into the freshwater Lake Ijssel and 2260 square kilometres of new land in five huge polders. The Delta Project involved damming all but two exits of the Rhine, Maas and Scheldt. This scheme protects land from floods and created a freshwater reservoir and 150 square kilometres of new land.

▶ WHERE IS THE REMOTEST PLACE ON EARTH?

Only a fifth of the Earth's land surface is densely populated, so there are still plenty of remote places. The remotest inhabited land is Tristan da Cunha, a volcanic island in the South Atlantic. The nearest inhabited land is over 2000 kilometres away.

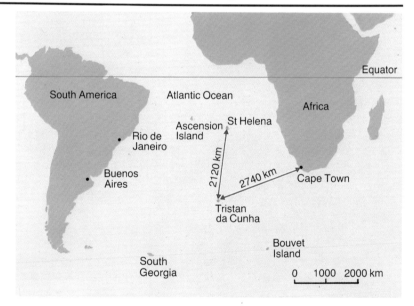

Four-fifths of the Earth's land surface is too dry, too cold, too mountainous or too densely forested to support many people. The most sparsely populated continent is Antarctica, which has no permanent settlement. The most sparsely populated country is Greenland.

The remotest island is Bouvet Island, an uninhabited Norwegian dependency in the South Atlantic. The nearest land is 1700 kilometres away, and that is the uninhabited coast of Antarctica.

The remotest inhabited island, Tristan da Cunha, covers just 98 square kilometres. Its nearest inhabited land is the island of St Helena, 2120 kilometres to the north-east.

In 1961 Tristan da Cunha erupted and all its inhabitants were evacuated, but they returned in 1963. Although the island looks lonely, they are happy there. Loneliness is often worse in great cities than in remote places.

▲ WHERE IS THE LARGEST ARTIFICIAL LAKE?

The artificial lake with the greatest area is Lake Volta in Ghana, West Africa. The Bratsk Reservoir on the Angara River in the USSR holds the greatest volume of water in an artificial lake.

In 1965, the Akosombo Dam was completed across the River Volta. The dam is built at the southern end of a gorge, and produces hydro-electric power.

Lake Volta began to build up behind the dam in the valley of the River Volta and its main headwaters, the Black Volta and the White Volta. Altogether the lake now covers 8482 square kilometres and its shoreline is 7250 kilometres long. Villagers had to move from the flooded area to the new shoreline, where they began a fishing industry.

Lake Volta is large but fairly shallow. In places, the remains of flooded forests stick out of the water. Its total volume is 148 cubic kilometres – compared to 169.25 cubic kilometres for the USSR's Bratsk Reservoir.

▲ WHERE IS THE BIGGEST MAN-MADE HOLE ON EARTH?

The largest modern quarry, excavated by machine, is Bingham Canyon Copper Mine, shown here, in Utah in the USA. It covers 7.2 square kilometres and is 774 metres deep.
The 'Big Hole' of Kimberley in South Africa is an old diamond mine which was dug out last century by thousands of miners working with only picks and shovels. It is about 500 metres in diameter and nearly 400 metres deep.

In 1871 diamonds were found on a farm which became the site of Kimberley Mine. By 1872 more than 3500 men claimed patches of land where they could dig for diamonds. As they dug out the pipe of kimberlite rock, they made a huge hole. Over 25 million tonnes of rock were dug out, yielding about three tonnes of diamonds.

Open mining stopped when rock falls became too frequent. The mine closed in 1915 and is now half full of water.

▲ WHERE DOES ACID RAIN OCCUR?

All rain is very slightly acid, but over the industrial areas of North America and Europe the rain is more acid because it absorbs waste gases which pollute the atmosphere.

Rainwater reacts with the carbon dioxide in the air to become a very dilute carbonic acid. This weak acid can dissolve limestone, which is an alkaline rock.

Rain can also react with the waste gases emitted into the air by factories, power stations and cars. Such gases may be carried great distances by winds and then fall as dilute sulphuric acid and nitric acid, often on areas far away from the source of pollution. This is called acid rain because its acidity is artificially high.

Acid rain increases the erosion of rocks and building materials, especially limestone. Lakes and streams are slowly poisoned, threatening wildlife. The face of the statue shown in the photograph above has been eaten away by acid rain.

◄ WHERE IS RICE GROWN?

Rice provides food for more people than any other cereal crop in the world. It is the basic food crop in much of southern and eastern Asia.

Rice needs hot weather and plenty of water. The water may come from heavy rain, such as the monsoon rains of Asia, or from irrigation. Rice needs flat land, because the water level in the fields must be carefully controlled. Many hillsides in Asia are terraced to get enough flat land. Some terraces are hundreds of years old.

The seedlings are grown in a 'nursery' bed and then transplanted to the flooded paddyfields. After four to five months the rice is ready for harvest and the water is released.

Rice is now grown in many hot, wet parts of the world apart from Asia. Mechanized rice-fields in the USA and southern Europe grow rice for export. Rice is also an important food crop in Egypt, West Africa, Madagascar and parts of South America.

► WHERE DOES COTTON COME FROM?

The cotton thread we sew with or weave into cloth is spun from fibres in the cotton boll. This is the seed pod of the cotton plant.

The cotton bush is an annual plant. It grows quickly and flowers, then small green seedpods develop. The seeds inside the cotton boll are surrounded by a mass of fine hairs. When the boll is ripe, it bursts open and the soft white cotton can be picked.

Once the cotton crop is harvested, it has to be ginned. This process separates the cotton fibre from the seeds so that the fibres can be cleaned, carded and spun.

Cotton was a major crop in south-eastern USA. Many Africans were imported as slaves to work on the cotton plantations. The USA still produces nearly a fifth of the world's cotton. Egypt and Sudan also export cotton. It is important too in parts of East Africa, India and Pakistan, China and parts of South America.

► WHERE IS TEA GROWN?

The tea we drink is made from the crushed leaves of an evergreen bush which grows in hot, damp climates. It seems to thrive at quite high altitudes, up to 2300 metres, in tropical areas.

Tea was first brought to Europe from China. As the drink became fashionable, plantations of tea bushes were planted by the Dutch in Indonesia and by the British in India and Sri Lanka. Now tea plantations are also found in Japan, in East Africa and on hillsides in Georgia in the USSR.

The tea plant needs a warm climate with plenty of moisture and a rich, well-drained soil. On tea plantations, the bush is pruned to a maximum height of 1.5 metres so it is easy to pick. The young leaves at the tops of the stems are picked. These are taken to a factory on the plantation where they are spread out to wither. They are then rolled and left to ferment. Heating and drying seals in the flavour and the tea is packed for export.

▶ WHERE DOES RUBBER COME FROM?

Natural rubber is made from latex, which is found under the bark of the rubber tree. This tree is a native of the Amazon rain forest and grows in hot, wet equatorial conditions.

Amazon Indians first collected latex from trees to make a type of rubber. Goodyear discovered how to harden rubber in 1842. When bicycles and cars became popular there was a great demand for rubber and the Amazon became a boom area.

The rubber tree was introduced to South-East Asia via London's botanical gardens at Kew. Plantations in Malaysia and Indonesia have supplied much of the world's rubber. Smaller amounts come from Zaire and West Africa.

The bark of the rubber tree is cut and the latex oozes into a cup fixed by the rubber tapper. The latex is then smoked and vulcanized to make rubber.

Nowadays, much of our rubber is synthetic and is a by-product of oil.

◀ WHERE WAS MAIZE FIRST GROWN?

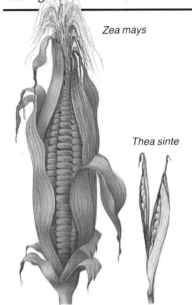

Zea mays

Thea sinte

Maize is an important cereal crop which is now grown in many parts of the world which have hot summers. It is a native of the Americas, and was an important food crop for many Indian tribes before Europeans arrived.

The origin of the modern maize plant (*Zea mays*) is still a mystery. It is an annual plant which now depends on humans for planting. It may be related to *Thea sinte*, a grass which grows in Mexico and whose cobs look very like miniature corn cobs. This plant can reproduce in the wild.

It is possible to cross *Thea sinte* with maize to develop fatter cobs. These look very like corn cobs found by archaeologists in New Mexico which may be 2000 years old.

For the early European settlers in America, 'Indian corn' was often a life-saver. Most American maize is now used as cattle food, but some is eaten as sweetcorn or turned into cornflakes or flour.

◀ WHERE DOES COCOA COME FROM?

Cocoa is made from the beans which develop in the large pod of the cacao tree. Cocoa was drunk by the Aztecs of Central America before Europeans arrived. The cacao tree is still grown in hot, wet areas of Central and South America, but most of the world's cocoa now comes from West Africa.

The tropical cacao tree grows in hot, wet, forested areas near the Equator. Large pods, 15-35 centimetres long, grow directly out of its branches and trunk. Each pod contains 30-40 beans. The beans are fermented and dried, and then exported for processing into cocoa and chocolate.

The Spanish *conquistadores* liked the bitter cocoa drink they found in Central America, and by the 17th century other Europeans had developed a taste for cocoa. It was the British and French who introduced cacao trees to West Africa, which is now the world's principal cocoa-producing region.

▲ WHERE IS MONUMENT VALLEY?

Monument Valley is part of the Colorado Plateau, in the dry south-west of the USA. The towers, columns and castle-like masses of rock are completely natural monuments.

The rocks of Monument Valley are mainly sandstones with some other sedimentary rocks. These rocks were pushed into an upfold or anticline. As this happened, the layers were stretched and weakened. Faults developed at the edges of the area. Lakes filled the faulted area, and rivers flowed along weaknesses in the rocks. As the rocks were uplifted the river deepened their valleys.

Over millions of years, many metres of rock have been eroded away. More resistant rocks have been left standing as columns and as islands of rock called 'buttes'. The toppled remains of columns litter the floor. Today, the climate is desert and the area is dry, but wind and flash-floods continue to erode the area.

▼ WHERE IS THERE SNOW NEAR THE EQUATOR?

Snow lies on the ground all year in places where the temperature is low enough to prevent it melting completely. Although it is hot at sea level at the Equator, it can get very cold indeed at the top of high mountains. Some Equatorial mountains are high enough to have permanent snow and ice, such as Mount Kilimanjaro in East Africa and the peaks of the Andes in Ecuador.

Mount Kilimanjaro is a volcano rising high above the East African plains on the borders of Kenya and Tanzania. The highest point is 5894 metres above sea level.

The place where permanent snow begins is called the snowline. The height of the snowline depends on the temperature and the amount of snow falling. Near the Poles, the snowline is at ground level. At latitude 40° the snowline is at 2500-5000 metres depending on the dryness of the climate. At the Equator, the snowline i a little over 5000 metres.

▲ WHERE IS THE GIANT'S CAUSEWAY?

The Giant's Causeway is on the north coast of Northern Ireland. It is a wavecut platform backed by high basalt cliffs. This once-molten rock formed a mass of columns as it cooled. According to Celtic legend, the giant Finn MacCool (or Fingal) built the Causeway to link Ireland to Scotland. Similar basalt formations are found in Scotland such as the Isle of Staffa where the sea carved Fingal's Cave.

Sixty million years ago a series of basalt lava flows began to cover large areas of northern Ireland and western Scotland. The lava cooled quickly, forming a dark rock. As it cooled and shrank, joints formed in a fairly regular pattern, giving rise to a vast number of hexagonal columns.

Most of the columns are vertical and form spectacular cliffs over 160 metres high. On the beach the columns have been eroded by the sea. They form amazing steps and pavements, projecting out into the sea towards Scotland.

▼ WHERE IS WAVE ROCK?

Wave Rock is in Western Australia, about 300 kilometres inland from Perth. It is a great granite rock, 15 metres high, which curves over like an incredible giant wave.

Wave Rock is part of a larger granite area called Hyden Rocks. The nearest settlement is Hyden, a tiny place with fewer than 200 people. Among the nearby granite formations are rocks known locally as Hippo's Yawn, King Rocks and The Humps.

The rock of which Wave Rock is made is about 2700 million years old. It is one of the rocks which form the ancient base of Australia. Today, the famous formation is coloured with vertical streaks which range from deep grey to red, ochre and sandy tints. These colours are the result of staining by various oxides.

The area around Wave Rock is very dry. Visitors can also explore the wildlife reserve around the rock which has many plants and animals native to Australia.

▲ WHERE IS 'OLD FAITHFUL'?

'Old Faithful' is one of many geysers and hot springs in Yellowstone National Park in the west of the USA. It got its name because it used to send a jet of steaming water 30 metres up into the air faithfully every 66 minutes. It is not quite so regular today.

Geysers occur when water seeps down through rock layers and is heated up by volcanic activity. The super-heated water is converted into high pressure steam which spurts out of the ground as a geyser.

The whole of Yellowstone National Park is located above a lava-filled hole in the Earth's crust. There was once a volcano here, which erupted so violently that the crater was blown apart and the whole area collapsed into the caldera, the remains of the crater.

This part of the USA receives heavy winter snowfalls, so there is a lot of water which is kept simmering on or just below the surface of the Earth.

PLANTS AND ANIMALS

Plants and animals tend to live in communities. Major communities are known as biomes. The world's biomes include coniferous forest, deciduous forest, grassland, desert, tundra and mountains.

Biomes are identified by the types of plant life they contain. The most important factor that determines plant life is climate. Temperature, wind and rainfall work together so that only certain kinds of plants can live in a particular area.

At the Poles, temperatures are so low that no plant life can survive. But slightly nearer the Equator there is a sparse vegetation known as tundra. This is followed by coniferous forest, of which there is a broad band in the northern hemisphere. Nearer still to the Equator, there are areas of deciduous forest. In dry regions this gives way to grassland, and in very dry areas only desert plants can survive. On the other hand there is tropical rain forest in areas that have high rainfall.

Every biome supports its own kinds of animals. But there is another factor that determines the types of animals and plants found in different places. The past and present geography of the world has resulted in many species being restricted to certain regions. For example, lions are found only in Africa.

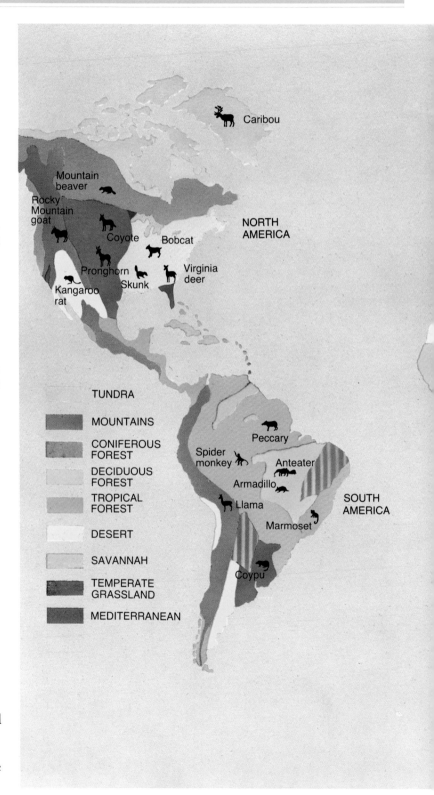

TUNDRA

MOUNTAINS

CONIFEROUS FOREST

DECIDUOUS FOREST

TROPICAL FOREST

DESERT

SAVANNAH

TEMPERATE GRASSLAND

MEDITERRANEAN

38

▼ WHY ARE SOME ANIMALS FOUND ONLY IN CERTAIN REGIONS?

Seas, mountains and deserts form natural barriers to the spread of animals.

The map below shows some of the animals that are confined to particular parts of the world. South America and Australia have unique mammals because these lands were cut off by the sea from the rest of the world during the evolution of the mammals. In other areas, the spread of mammals has been limited by such things as climate, and the presence of deserts and mountain ranges.

EUROPE

Red squirrel

Northern lynx

Brown hare

Roe deer

Saiga antelope

Dormouse

Wild boar

Hedgehog

Bactrian camel

Jerboa

ASIA

Yak

Panda

Mongoose

Tiger

Addax

Fennec

AFRICA

Flying lemur

Giraffe

Lion

Tree shrew

Chimpanzee

Orang-utan

Hippopotamus

Vervet monkey

Kangaroo

Golden mole

Dingo

Koala

Gemsbok

Platypus

AUSTRALIA

▶ WHERE DO PENGUINS BREED?

All penguins live in the southern hemisphere. A number of them breed in Antarctic and sub-Antarctic areas.

Penguins spend most of their time at sea, but they all come ashore to breed. Only two, the emperor and Adélie penguins, breed on the Antarctic coast.

Emperor penguins, which are the largest penguins of all, breed in the perpetual darkness of the Antarctic winter. They gather in large 'rookeries' on the ice and do not build nests. The males incubate the eggs for two months. Adélie penguins begin nesting in September and October, during the Antarctic spring. They make nests of pebbles on the beaches.

Emperor penguin

Chinstrap penguin   Macaroni penguin   Gentoo penguin

King, macaroni, chinstrap and gentoo penguins breed on sub-Antarctic islands. The king penguin is closely related to the emperor but, like the Adélie, it breeds on stony beaches in the Antarctic spring. The male and female take turns at incubating the egg.

The remaining 11 species all breed farther north. Some, such as the rockhopper penguin, breed on Southern Ocean islands. Others are found on continental coasts.

▶ WHICH SEALS LIVE IN THE ANTARCTIC?

Only four true seals breed in Antarctic waters. They are the crabeater seal, the Weddell seal, the Ross seal and the leopard seal.

Each species of Antarctic seal has its own specialized way of life. Crabeater seals live along the coasts and feed on krill, which they filter from the water using specially adapted teeth.

Ross seals, the smallest of the Antarctic seals, are usually seen on the pack ice and seem to be strong, agile swimmers. They eat squid, fish and krill. Ross seals have been known to play with killer whales, their natural enemies, while feeding on squid.

Weddell seals live along the coasts and are the most placid of the Antarctic seals. They

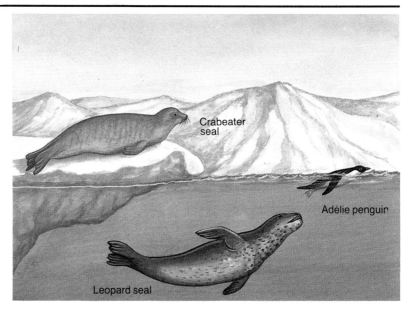

Crabeater seal

Adélie penguin

Leopard seal

feed on fish such as Antarctic cod and icefish, and are known for their diving skills. They can dive down to over 300 metres and stay submerged for over 40 minutes. Their blood and circulatory system are specially adapted for this. Ice covers their feeding areas in winter. Weddell seals make holes in the ice so that they can come up for air.

Leopard seals are the most carnivorous of the Antarctic seals. They live along the edge of the pack ice and feed on fish, penguins and even the cubs of other seals.

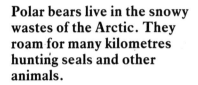

Polar bear

Ringed seal

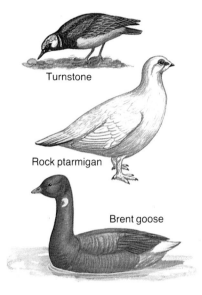

Turnstone

Rock ptarmigan

Brent goose

Wolf

Arctic hare

Reindeer (caribou)

▲ WHERE ARE POLAR BEARS FOUND?

Polar bears live in the snowy wastes of the Arctic. They roam for many kilometres hunting seals and other animals.

Polar bears are found farther north than any other land mammal. In winter they range across the pack ice of the Arctic Ocean. There they hunt seals, particularly ringed seals, which they capture with great skill. They also eat young walruses and stranded whales.

In spring and summer, polar bears are carried south by the ice. In the tundra they eat plant material such as lichen, moss, grass and berries. Polar bears are good swimmers, although they usually avoid large stretches of open water. They walk with ease across the ice floes because their feet have hairy, non-slip soles.

Polar bears mate in the spring and the cubs are born in December or January. The female gives birth inside a 'maternity den' dug into a bank of snow.

▲ WHICH BIRDS NEST IN THE ARCTIC?

Over 100 types of bird nest in the Arctic in summer. Only a few remain during winter.

The Arctic summer lasts only about three months. But during this time many birds nest and rear their young.

Among the summer visitors are ducks, such as long-tailed ducks, geese, such as Brent geese, and swans. They all come to feed on the rich summer vegetation of the tundra wetlands. Insect larvae attract wading birds such as phalaropes, turnstones, knots and dunlins. Flying insects attract warblers, wheatears, fieldfares and yellowhammers. Arctic terns and skuas feed on fish.

As summer ends, many birds fly south to avoid the harsh Arctic winter. Of those that remain, the rock ptarmigan moults its brown feathers and becomes totally white. It shelters in burrows tunnelled into the snow. Other birds that spend winter in the Arctic include the snowy owl, raven, gyr falcon, peregrine falcon and the redpoll.

▲ WHERE DO CARIBOU LIVE?

The caribou of North America, together with a number of other mammals, range across the tundra wastes. Reindeer are a semi-domesticated variety of caribou found in northern Europe and Asia.

Caribou and musk oxen are the large herbivores (plant-eaters) of the tundra. In summer they range across the tundra, feeding on many kinds of plants. Their main enemies are wolves and sometimes grizzly bears. Smaller carnivores (flesh-eaters) include foxes and weasels. These hunt shrews, lemmings, ground squirrels and the Arctic hare.

In winter, caribou move south and feed on reindeer moss (a type of lichen), and the twigs of trees such as birch and aspen. Musk oxen remain farther north. In the coldest weather they huddle together to keep warm.

Small mammals tunnel beneath the snow. There they are protected from the biting winds. They feed on seeds and dry grass.

41

Bighorn sheep are found in the Rocky Mountains. They, and the Rocky Mountain goats which also inhabit this region, are agile climbers.

North America has three main mountain ranges. In the east the Appalachians stretch from Labrador to Georgia. In the west there are the coastal ranges that form the Pacific Rim, and the Rocky Mountains which stretch from Alaska to Mexico.

Many animals live in these mountains. Bighorn sheep are sure-footed and scramble among the rocks with ease. Rocky Mountain goats are an American form of goat-antelope. In addition to these animals, there are mountain lions (cougars), Canadian lynxes, beavers, the hoary marmot and the jack rabbit, and many small rodents. Mule deer are found on the lower slopes.

There are also vultures such as the red-headed turkey vulture, and birds of prey such as the golden eagle, bald eagle and osprey.

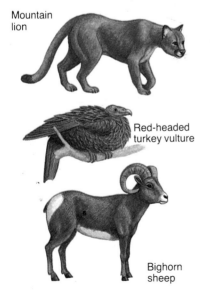

Mountain lion

Red-headed turkey vulture

Bighorn sheep

Ibexes are wild goats. The seven types of ibex are all found in the mountains of Europe, Asia and North Africa. The European species are the Spanish ibex and the Alpine ibex.

The three mountain ranges of Europe – the Carpathians, Alps and Pyrenees – are all relics of the last Ice Age. When the glaciers retreated, these mountains were left as cold 'islands' in a much warmer Europe.

Ring ouzel

Golden eagle

Ibex

Marmot

Ibexes are excellent climbers. They sometimes use their dew claws (at the back of each foot) to give them extra grip. Two other cloven-hooved mountain animals are the mouflon (a wild sheep) and the chamois (a goat-antelope).

Other alpine animals include lynxes, marmots and susliks (European ground squirrels). The Pyrenees are home to the Pyrenean desman, a water-living relative of the mole. Alpine birds include the alpine chough, ring ouzel, wallcreeper and birds of prey such as the golden eagle.

The yak is the largest of the Himalayan mammals. Wild herds live on the high plateaus of Tibet. Domesticated yak are found all over the highlands of Central Asia.

The Himalayas are home to a number of unique animals. As well as the yak there are several hooved animals such as the Tibetan wild ass, the tahr, markhor, bharal and the largest of all living sheep, the argali. The Siberian ibex is the main prey of the beautiful and rare snow leopard. Smaller animals include the alpine marmot and the high-mountain vole. The large-eared pika is unusual because it does not hibernate during the winter. Instead it lives in its burrow, feeding on hay and other dried plants gathered during the summer.

Himalayan birds include choughs, ravens and the Himalayan snow partridge. Carrion-eaters such as the lammergeier vulture, Himalayan griffon and black vulture, are common.

Lammergeier vulture

Snow leopard

Markhor

Yak

▼ WHERE DO PANDAS LIVE?

East of the Himalayas lies Szechwan, in the highlands of south-west China. High in these mountains are the bamboo thickets in which pandas live.

The valleys of Szechwan contain subtropical habitats. These change to broadleaved woodland, coniferous woodland and alpine habitats towards the snow-capped peaks of the mountains. Between 1800 and 2500 metres above sea level, the coniferous forest is broken by thickets of bamboo and rhododendron. Here the giant panda lives. It feeds on bamboo shoots and other plants, and even eats small animals occasionally.

The red, or lesser, panda is also found in this region. It too feeds on leaves and fruit, but it is not closely related to the giant panda.

Szechwan is the home of three goat-antelopes – the takin, goral and serow. There are also primitive shrews such as the mole shrew, the web-footed water shrew and the Himalayan water shrew.

▼ WHERE DO LLAMAS LIVE?

The llama is the domesticated pack animal of the High Andes in South America. Its close relatives are the alpaca, guanaco and vicuna.

The Indians of the High Andes domesticated the llama over 4000 years ago. The llama and the alpaca are thought to have been bred from the guanaco. Vicunas and guanacos have never been domesticated. All these animals are well-adapted for life where the air is thin.

Torrent duck

Spectacled bear

Llama

They have large lungs and extra red blood-cells.

The northern part of the Andes has high plains. These are home to many animals, including the spectacled bear, South American mountain tapir, and deer such as the Ecuadorian pudu and the Andean deer, or guemel.

Many birds also inhabit the High Andes. The Andean condor soars high among the peaks. The sierra finch builds its nest among the spiny leaves of puya plants, and torrent ducks live in the tumbling streams.

▼ WHERE ARE THE STRANGEST MOUNTAIN PLANTS FOUND?

Some mountainous regions have very unusual plants. In the mountains of Africa there are giant lobelias and tree groundsels. The Andes have giant lupins and bromeliads. The Chilean pine, or monkey puzzle tree, is one of the few remaining southern conifers.

Mountain plants must survive extreme cold. They are usually low-growing, creeping or cushion-forming plants. However, the giant plants of Africa and South America are extraordinary exceptions.

Giant lobelias and tree groundsels grow to about six metres in height. Their leaves are arranged so that they close up at night into 'buds'. The undersides of the leaves also have a covering of thick, felty hair to protect the 'buds' from the cold.

The giant plants of the Andes are similar. One of the most spectacular is the giant puya, *Puya raymondii*. This has a palm-like trunk, a rosette of long leaves and a tall spike of bird-pollinated flowers.

Monkey puzzle tree

Giant lupin

Giant groundsel

43

NORTH AMERICAN
BOREAL FOREST

Tengmalm's
owl

Larch

Lodgepole
pine

Great
horned owl

Sitka
spruce

Flying
squirrel

Chickaree

Moose

Wolverine

Brown bear

Chipmunk

Virginia
opossum

Mink

Ground squirrel

▲ WHERE DO MOST
CONIFERS GROW?

**Below the tundra of the
northern hemisphere there is
a broad band of poor soils
left behind after the last Ice
Age. In these cold regions
the land is mostly covered
with coniferous forest.**

The habitat provided by the
world's northern coniferous
forests is known as taiga. The
North American boreal
(northern) forest, which is
shown above, contains trees
such as white and black

spruce, sitka spruce, lodgepole
pine and tamarack (a larch). In
wet areas a few deciduous
trees, such as aspen, willow
and birch, are found.

In the coniferous forest of
northern Europe, the main
trees are Norway spruce and
Scots pine. But farther east in
the Siberian taiga (shown on
the opposite page) the forest
becomes more varied. Here the
most commonly found conifers
include Siberian fir, Siberian
larch, stone pine and Siberian
spruce. Forest fires are
common, so many areas of the
Eurasian taiga are at different

stages of growth. In the newly
burned areas birches and
aspens are the most common
tree. The Eurasian taiga is the
world's largest forest. It is
about one third larger than the
whole of the USA.

Few herbaceous (non-
woody) plants grow in the taiga
because it is too cold and too
dark (the conifers shut out
much of the light). Also, the
decomposing conifer needles
produce a very acid humus.
Many kinds of fungi help
break down the humus, and
some plants do survive in
clearings.

SIBERIAN TAIGA

Pine marten

Ural owl

Stone pine

Goosander

Siberian fir

Siberian tit

Siberian rubythroat

Crossbill

Varying hare

Northern lynx

Waxwing

Capercaillie

Hazel hen

Wood lemming

◄ WHICH BIRDS LIVE IN CONIFEROUS FORESTS?

The northern forests provide food for many seed-eating and insect-eating birds. Hawks and owls hunt small birds and mammals.

During the summer vast swarms of aphids, mosquitoes and other insects appear in the taiga and provide food for migrant birds such as warblers. Resident insect-eaters include woodpeckers and tits.

Seed-eating birds are also very common. These include the crossbill, the Siberian jay and the pine grosbeak. Waxwings feed on berries as well as seeds. Members of the grouse family, such as the capercaillie, hazel hen and spruce grouse (in North America), feed on seeds, leaves, buds and berries.

Predatory birds include the great horned owl of North America and the Ural owl of Siberia, and a few hawks such as the goshawk. Two unusual taiga birds are the goldeneye and goosander ducks, which nest in abandoned woodpecker holes in trees.

▲ WHICH MAMMALS LIVE IN CONIFEROUS FORESTS?

The coniferous forests of North America and Eurasia support both herbivores and carnivores. The herbivores feed on the leaves, seeds and bark of the trees, and they are hunted by the carnivores. Similar but different species have evolved in each region.

The largest herbivore of the North American forest is the moose (known as the elk in Eurasia) which feeds on low-growing plants and the leaves of deciduous trees. Caribou also venture into the forest during the winter.

Seed-eating mammals include ground squirrels, tree squirrels (such as the grey squirrel), the golden chipmunk, the spruce mouse and the Virginia opossum. Flying squirrels and the chickaree (an American red squirrel) feed on pine cones and toadstools as well as on the eggs and nestlings of small birds. North American tree-porcupines feed on catkins and leaves. In winter they strip the bark off trees and can cause a lot of damage.

The carnivores of the North American forest include the wolf, brown bear, black bear, American mink and wolverine.

Similar animals are found in the Siberian taiga. Here we find the elk, the brown bear, the Siberian chipmunk, the wood lemming, the Siberian weasel, the sable and the pine marten. There are also flying squirrels, ground squirrels and tree squirrels such as the European red squirrel. The northern lynx eats hares, and the wolverine eats northern red-backed voles.

▶ WHY IS DECIDUOUS
WOODLAND SO RICH IN
WILDLIFE?

Deciduous forests contain a fine undergrowth of small trees, shrubs and herbaceous (non-woody) plants. Such a variety of plants provides food for many animals.

Deciduous forest once covered the entire northern temperate region. Today, in this region, there are only three principal areas of deciduous woodland. The most varied woodland is found in eastern Asia, which has magnolias, tulip trees, sweet gums, planes, horse chestnuts, oaks, beeches, hickories and hornbeams, to name just a few. Many of these trees also grow in the woodlands of eastern North America, although fewer species are found there. European woodlands contain only about 20 species. The main types include oak, ash, beech, hornbeam, field maple, birch and alder.

Deciduous woodland consists of several layers of vegetation. The top layer is formed by tall trees; then come smaller trees and a layer of shrubs such as holly, honeysuckle, blackthorn, elder and hazel. Below this there is a layer of herbaceous plants such as bluebell, primrose and dog's mercury. Finally there is a ground layer, consisting of mosses and other small plants.

The leaves of all these plants are much less tough than the needles of conifers, so they attract a large number of plant-eating animals. The wealth of seeds and fruits also attracts plant-eaters. In turn, many predatory animals feed on the plant-eaters.

▶ WHICH ANIMALS LIVE IN
DECIDUOUS FORESTS?

Plant-eating woodland animals range from large species such as deer to small ones such as mice and voles. Predators include foxes and weasels.

Large European herbivores include the red deer, roe deer, fallow deer and wild boar. In North America the whitetail deer, which was once almost wiped out by hunters, is now increasing in numbers.

Smaller European plant-eaters include the red squirrel, the dormouse, bank vole, wood mouse, hedgehog and rabbit. In America there are similar animals, such as the grey squirrel, eastern chipmunk, white-footed mouse and the pine vole.

The largest predators, such as the wolf, the lynx (in Europe) and the mountain lion (in North America), have almost completely disappeared from deciduous woodland. Instead, today's main predators are foxes such as the European red fox and the North American red and grey foxes. In America other predators include the bobcat, the racoon, the ring-tailed cat, the skunk, the long-tailed weasel and the short-tailed shrew. European predators include the weasel, stoat, beech marten, polecat and pine marten. Badgers feed on plant material, as well as small animals.

Invertebrate animals play a vital part in the life of deciduous woodland. Worms, beetles and ants help to break down the leaf litter into humus. Many insects are eaten by birds.

▶ WHICH BIRDS LIVE IN
DECIDUOUS FORESTS?

Enormous numbers of birds nest and feed in the world's deciduous forests. They feed on insects, seeds, berries, buds and leaves. Birds of prey feed on small birds and mammals.

A number of birds live all the year round in European deciduous woodland. Omnivorous species include the blackbird, which feeds on insects, worms and berries; the song thrush, which enjoys snails; and the jay, which eats eggs and nestlings and sometimes mice and lizards. The chaffinch feeds on small seeds and insects, as do the wren and the goldfinch. The hawfinch feeds on fruit stones and large seeds. Tits, such as the great tit and blue tit, feed mainly on insects but also eat berries and seeds. Woodpeckers search for insects under pieces of loose bark, and treecreepers dig insects out of small crevices. The wood pigeon feeds on leaves, buds and seeds.

Summer visitors include the nightingale, which feeds mainly on ground insects. The nightjar catches flying insects with its wide-open mouth. Other summer visitors include flycatchers, warblers and the turtle dove.

Woodland birds of prey include the sparrowhawk, kite and buzzard. Tawny owls hunt by night.

American woodland contains a similar range of birds. It includes several woodpeckers and the striking blue jay. Summer visitors include a number of warblers, vireos and tanagers.

EUROPEAN DECIDUOUS WOODLAND

Tawny owl

Sparrowhawk

Greater spotted woodpecker

Blue tit

Green woodpecker

Jay

Lacewing

Gall wasp

Fallow deer

Red fox

Wild boar

Roe deer

Tortoise moth

Stoat

Hedgehog

Badger

Rabbit

Dormouse

NORTH AMERICAN DECIDUOUS WOODLAND

Bobcat

Scarlet tanager

Red-headed woodpecker

Blue jay

Whitetail deer

Grey squirrel

Grey fox

Red-eyed vireo

Skunk

Eastern chipmunk

Racoon

47

▼ WHERE DO COYOTES LIVE?

The North American prairies lie between the Mississippi River and the Rocky Mountains. They are the home of a number of plant-eating animals. The coyote is one of the main predators.

The grey wolf was once common on the North American prairies, but it has largely been replaced by the smaller and highly successful coyote, or prairie wolf. The coyote's prey includes jack rabbits, cottontails, prairie dogs and other rodents. It also eats carrion (the carcasses of dead animals).

Coyotes are well-known for their 'singing'. In the evening two or three coyotes may 'sing' together – an eerie sound that has given rise to many legends.

Other predators include the mountain lion, the black-footed ferret and the American badger. The favourite food of the American badger is the prairie dog. American badgers can burrow underground with amazing speed. Unlike European badgers, they hunt by day as well as by night.

▼ WHERE DO PRAIRIE DOGS MAKE THEIR HOMES?

Prairie dogs are so called because of their short barking calls. They dig underground burrows in large colonies on the North American prairies. Prairie dogs are rodents belonging to the squirrel family.

Prairie dogs' colonies, or 'towns', can be very large. In 1901 one colony was estimated to cover an area 160 by 380 kilometres. It is thought to have contained about 400 million animals. Today, however, prairie-dog towns are much smaller.

Each town is divided into a number of wards. These, in turn, are divided into coteries, which form the basic family unit. Members of the same coterie groom each other and feed together, and chase off outsiders.

Prairie dogs feed on grasses and other small, fast-growing plants. They have many predators, but an alarm call from one prairie dog is enough to send all those within earshot running for their burrows. It is usually only the sick, slow or unwary that get caught.

▼ WHAT HAPPENED TO THE BISON?

Large herds of bison and pronghorns once roamed the North American prairies. But during the 1800s hunters almost wiped them out.

The American bison is descended from the Asian bison (now extinct) which crossed into America via the Bering land bridge that existed a million years ago. At one time there were probably about 50 million plains bison in North America, but by 1889 there were only 540 left. The rest had been slaughtered for their meat, bones or hides – and often simply for sport. However, since the bison became a protected animal, numbers have increased and there are now several thousand in national parks.

The story of the pronghorn is a similar one. About 20 million years ago, there were probably over 40 million of these animals. In the 1800s, European settlers hunted them in great numbers and by 1925 there were only about 30,000 pronghorns left. But they have now grown in number to about 400,000.

Coyote

Bison

Pronghorn

American badger

Prairie dogs

The South American pampas is the home of some unique animals. These include armadillos and the viscacha, mara and aperea.

The temperate grassland known as the pampas is found on the plains of Argentina and Uruguay. Here it is possible to travel hundreds of kilometres without seeing a tree.

There are few large herbivores. The rare pampas deer is the largest, and there are occasional herds of guanaco.

Small herbivores include a number of South America's unique range of rodents. Viscachas tunnel labyrinth-like towns underground. The mara, or Patagonian hare, digs deep burrows. This animal is also found farther south on the dry Patagonian steppe, and manages to live without drinking. Other grassland rodents include the pampas guinea-pig, or aperea, and the tuco-tuco. The aperea does not burrow. Instead it hides in tufts of grass.

Several armadillos are found in the pampas. They include the nine-banded, giant, hairy, and fairy armadillos. The giant anteater also roams the plains.

Pampas predators include the southern grey fox, the long-legged maned wolf and the rare pampas cat.

Pampas birds include the rhea, the rufous ovenbird and the burrowing owl, which is also found in the dry areas of North America. There are also some species of tinamou. These are shy, partridge-like birds that can fly, but rarely take to the air.

Grassland occurs in those parts of the world where the rainfall is low or very seasonal. Fires and grazing animals help to prevent trees from growing.

Some temperate parts of the world, especially the centres of large continents, receive most of their rain at particular times of the year. In summer such areas have dry, hot weather and in winter there is often a thick covering of snow.

Trees find it difficult to grow in these conditions and so the land is mainly covered with grasses mixed with small herbaceous plants. Fires are common during the dry season and these help to keep down the trees. Grazing animals also help to maintain temperate grassland, as they nibble off the young shoots of any trees before they can grow.

Temperate grasslands include the steppes of central Asia, the North American prairies, the South American pampas and the South African veld.

Guanaco

Rhea

Maned wolf

Pampas deer

Hairy armadillo

Rufous ovenbird

Cavy

Viscacha

▶ WHAT IS SAVANNAH?

Savannah is tropical grassland. It occurs in hot regions where rainfall is very seasonal. The best-known savannah is that of Africa.

The African savannah is a dry, dusty region for most of the year, and the rainy season lasts for only four months. The most common grass is red oat-grass, and the savannah is also dotted with acacia and baobab trees. Some areas are fairly well wooded.

▶ WHICH BIRDS LIVE IN THE SAVANNAH?

The African savannah supports huge numbers of insect-eating and seed-eating birds. Among the most notable of African birds is the ostrich.

The huge, flightless ostrich is the world's largest living bird. It feeds on fruit, seeds and small animals. The savannah is also the home of the world's heaviest flying bird, the kori bustard, which may weigh over 50 kilograms. Bustards also feed on both plant material and animals.

Oxpeckers are common on the savannah. They perch on the backs of grazing animals, and feed on ticks and other parasites. Other savannah birds include bulbuls, shrikes, marabou storks, cranes and ground hornbills. Weaver birds build elaborate hanging nests in trees, as do their close relatives, the queleas. Huge flocks of queleas can cause a lot of damage to trees.

Birds of prey include the secretary bird and lanner falcon. Several types of vulture feed on the carcasses of dead animals.

Labels in image: Elephants, Giraffe, Gerenu, Zebras, Cheetah, Thomson's gazelle, Jackal, Griffon vulture, White-headed vulture

▲ WHICH SAVANNAH ANIMALS LIVE IN HERDS?

The savannah is populated with large, sometimes vast, herds of grazing hooved mammals. Zebras and wildebeests form some of the largest herds.

A lone antelope grazing on the savannah is open to attack. The chances of such an animal surviving are small. On the other hand, the members of a herd give each other some protection. They can warn each other of the presence of danger. An individual animal within a herd also stands a much greater chance of not being singled out by a predator. When a predator does attack, the milling, rushing herd may confuse it.

The most abundant hooved mammals are wildebeests, zebras, hartebeests and Thomson's gazelles. They normally live in small scattered herds, but during the calving season they gather together in larger herds for protection. At the start of the dry season they also migrate in vast herds to moister areas.

Weaver birds

Wildebeest

Ostriches

White rhino

Oxpecker

ant's gazelle

Lion

If all the savannah plant-eaters grazed in the same way, they would soon run out of food. But in fact each species feeds in a different way. In some cases the feeding method of one species actually helps another.

The herbivores of the savannah do not compete with each other for food. On the grassy plains of the Serengeti National Park, zebras chew off the coarse tops of grasses before moving on to another area. They are followed by wildebeests and topis, which eat the leafy centres of the plants almost down to the ground. Finally, Thomson's gazelles eat fallen seeds and young shoots at ground level. The gazelles benefit from the feeding of the earlier, larger animals. They can find their food easily because the tall grasses have been trampled and eaten.

In more wooded areas of savannah, competition for food is avoided in a similar way. Warthogs graze and also dig for bulbs and tubers on the ground. Springboks feed mainly on grass, but other antelopes are only partial grazers. They feed on the leaves and twigs of bushes and trees as well as on grass, and each species has its own preferred type of food. Dik-diks, steinboks, Grant's gazelles, kudus, elands and white rhinos browse increasingly higher levels of the bushes and trees. The topmost branches are browsed by elephants, which often destroy whole trees, and also by giraffes.

▲ WHICH ARE THE SAVANNAH HUNTERS?

Where there are so many plant-eating animals, there are naturally a number of predators. Each species of predator has its own method of hunting.

The best-known savannah hunter is the lion, the 'King of Beasts'. Lions often hunt in groups, or prides, and it is the lionesses who usually do the work of stalking and killing the prey.

The world's fastest animal, the cheetah, is also a savannah hunter. It approaches stealthily to within 100 metres or so of its prey and then runs it down by sheer speed. The leopard, on the other hand, prefers to lie in wait in a tree or among any suitable cover. The victim is then taken with a short, powerful charge.

Other savannah predators include the wild dog, serval, bat-eared fox, civet and banded mongoose. Jackals and hyenas hunt small animals. They are also scavengers, often taking over the abandoned kills of larger predators.

▼ WHERE IS THE DESERT COLD IN WINTER?

The deserts of Central Asia are baked dry during the summer. But in winter they are exposed to icy air from the Arctic. Even so, many animals survive there.

The Central Asian deserts stretch from the Caspian Sea eastwards to the Gobi Desert in Mongolia. Some of the most common animals are the jerboas, of which there are a number of species. Other rodents include the desert hedgehog and long-eared hedgehog. Large mammals are more common than in other deserts. The bactrian camel lives in the Gobi Desert. Wild asses and Mongolian gazelles (the most northerly of all gazelles) also roam the deserts of Asia. Snakes and lizards are very common. One of the largest desert snakes is the lebatine viper.

A number of birds can be found in the Asian deserts, particularly in spring, when food is plentiful. They include desert warblers, desert larks, stone curlews, desert shrikes, sandgrouse and hawks.

Eared agama

Jerboa

Grey monitor

Bactrian camel

▼ CAN FISH SURVIVE IN HOT WATER?

At the southern end of Death Valley in Nevada, USA, there is a series of small streams and lakes. These are the home of desert pupfish, which survive water temperatures that would kill most fish.

The streams and lakes these pupfish live in were once very

Cactus wren

Scott's oriole

Kit fox

Kangaroo rat

Cottontail

Burrowing owl

Night lizard

Western diamondback rattlesnake

Pupfish

▲ WHERE DO CACTI GROW?

Cacti are the most familiar of all desert plants. But they are not found in all deserts – only in those of North and South America. They help support a number of desert animals.

Pronghorns sometimes visit the desert to feed on cacti and shrubs, but most North American desert animals are much smaller. The kangaroo rat is a jumping rodent that burrows into the sandy ground and shelters in its burrow during the day. At night it comes out to feed on seeds and other plant material. It probably never drinks. Other small herbivores include the

large lakes. During the last Ice Age they covered much of what is now desert. Pupfish feed on the algae that grow in these warm waters. They can survive temperatures of just over 42°C.

The populations of the various species of pupfish were once numbered in tens of thousands. Today, however, predators and irrigation schemes have reduced their numbers.

desert cottontail, wood rat and grasshopper mouse. Desert hunters include the bobcat and the kit fox which resembles the Saharan fennec.

Amongst the many snakes and lizards are the American sidewinder, a rattlesnake, and the gila monster, one of the world's two poisonous lizards. Insect-eating birds include Scott's oriole, the cactus wren and the poor-will, which hibernates during the winter. Elf owls nest in abandoned woodpecker holes in saguaro cactus stems. The burrowing owl shares the underground homes of other animals, including, on occasions, rattlesnakes!

▼ WHICH IS THE WORLD'S LARGEST DESERT?

The world's largest desert is the Sahara Desert, which forms a broad band across North Africa. In most places the annual rainfall is less than 100 millimetres and it is one of the hottest places in the world.

Desert is often thought of as stretches of rolling sand dunes.

But, although the Sahara does contain seas of dunes (known as ergs), there are other types of desert as well. There are raised plateaus of rock known as hamadas, and large flat, stony regions known as regs.

Despite this bleak landscape, the Sahara is far from lifeless. Tough, hardy plants provide food for many insects such as beetles, grasshoppers and crickets. Even moths and butterflies appear after the occasional rainstorm. In turn, these insects are eaten by other animals such as lizards, snakes, scorpions, jerboas, gerbils, sand rats and desert hedgehogs. Larger animals include the fennec, which preys on small rodents, and the addax, a desert antelope. Desert birds include sandgrouse, larks and several species that fly in to feed on seeds and insects.

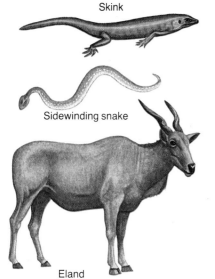

Skink

Sidewinding snake

Eland

Fat sand rat

Pintail sandgrouse

Lanner falcon

Fennec

Addax

▲ HOW DO DESERT ANIMALS SURVIVE?

The desert presents its inhabitants with several problems. The biggest of these are how to stay cool and how to get enough moisture. Desert animals have evolved a number of adaptations that enable them to survive.

Many desert animals have large ears, feet and tails. These are used as radiators to help get rid of excess heat. Large ears have an additional advantage. They enable their owners to hear the slightest sound in the still desert air. The hearing of the fennec, for example, is particularly keen.

Most desert animals shelter from the heat of the Sun during the day and are active only at night or in the early morning and evening. But some animals are out and about during the day. A desert locust keeps cool by turning its head towards the Sun, thus exposing the least possible area of its body to the searing heat.

Because water is scarce in the desert, animals have to make full use of the little they can get. Many desert animals do not sweat and they produce very concentrated urine and dry faeces. Large herbivores, which cannot shelter in burrows, have the greatest problem. The eland, which lives near the edge of the Sahara, manages to find some shelter and some water. But the addax and the oryx survive in the hottest areas without drinking. All their water is obtained from dew and the sparse plant-life. Few birds nest in the desert, though the sandgrouse is an exception. It flies long distances to find water, which it carries back to its nestlings by soaking its breast feathers.

Movement in sandy areas of desert is not easy. Many desert rodents are jumping rather than walking animals. The horned viper of the Sahara sidewinds across the sand and sandfish (types of skink) almost 'swim'.

▶ WHERE IS THE WORLD'S LARGEST RAIN FOREST?

Tropical rain forest occurs in warm, moist regions near the Equator. The largest area of rain forest is the Amazon basin in South America.

Of all the world's biomes, tropical rain forests contain the greatest variety of wildlife. This is because these areas receive an enormous amount of warmth, sunlight and rain. In the wettest areas plant growth, flowering and fruiting continues throughout the year. This kind of habitat provides homes and food for ten times the number of animals found in deciduous woodland.

Five layers can be seen in tropical forest. At ground level, fungi, mosses and ferns grow in the rich leaf litter. The second layer consists of tree ferns, shrubs and lianas. Next there is a layer of young tree crowns, and above this is the thick canopy, the crowns of mature trees. The topmost layer consists of the few trees that stand above the canopy.

Tropical rain forest contains a wealth of insect life. There are countless butterflies, beetles, mantises, stick insects and crickets. Many of these have amazing forms of camouflage. Others have bright warning colours or markings that are used to startle predators.

Amphibians and reptiles are also common. In the Amazon forest arrow poison frogs, tree frogs and horned frogs prey on insects and other small animals. Snakes include the anaconda, boa constrictor and coral snakes. Lizards include the green iguana, anole and tegu.

White-eared puffbird

Harpy eagle

Topaz hummingbird

Spectacled owl

Sulphur-breasted toucan

Gold and blue macaw

Paradise jacamar

Amazon parrot

Lovely cotinga

Gold-hooded manakin

Great curassow

Common marmoset

Red-mantled tamarin

Spider monkey

Howler monkey

Bird-eating spider

Leafcutter ant

▲ WHICH KINDS OF BIRD LIVE IN RAIN FOREST?

The canopy of any tropical rain forest provides food for a host of birds. Many feed on the nectar, fruits and seeds of the trees.

The brightly coloured birds of the Amazon forest blend with the luminous greens, reds and yellows of the flowers and foliage. Toucans, parrots, parakeets, macaws and curassows feed on the plentiful supply of fruit. Smaller fruit-eaters include manakins, cotingas and bellbirds. Insect-eaters include jacamars, puff-birds, trogons and tanagers. Hummingbirds and honeycreepers feed on nectar.

One of the strangest birds of the Amazon is the hoatzin, whose young have claws on their wings to help them scramble about the trees. One of the few birds of prey is the harpy eagle.

A similar range of birds can be found in the African rain forests. As in South America, there are a number of parrots, but in Africa hornbills take the place of toucans.

◄ WHICH MAMMALS LIVE IN THE AMAZON RAIN FOREST?

Tropical forests are inhabited by a large number of monkeys. The Amazon forest is also the home of sloths and other climbing mammals.

New World Monkeys abound in the Amazon forest. Troops of capuchins, titis, spider monkeys, woolly monkeys, squirrel monkeys, tamarins and marmosets (the smallest of all monkeys) spend their days in the forest canopy, searching for fruit, flowers and buds. Douroucoulis are the only ones that sleep during the day. Uakaris and sakis move around singly or in pairs. The largest of the South American monkeys are the howler monkeys, which set up a howling chorus just after sunrise to establish the whereabouts of rival groups.

Most of these monkeys have grasping, or prehensile, tails. This is also true of other South American forest animals, such as the Brazilian tree-porcupine, the kinkajou and the tamandua, or collared anteater. Other tree dwellers include the sloths. They hang from branches, using their huge claws, and move very slowly through the forest, feeding on leaves. Coatis are excellent climbers and eat almost anything that is edible, as does their relative the crab-eating racoon.

Rodents, such as acoushis and agoutis, forage on the forest floor, eating all kinds of plant material, especially fallen fruit and nuts. Forest hunters include the jaguar, ocelot, margay cat and tayra, a member of the weasel family.

Colobus monkey

Chimpanzee

Gorilla

Tree pangolin

Royal antelope

Bongo

Genet

Elephant shrew   Water chevrotain   Okapi

◄ WHICH MAMMALS LIVE IN AFRICAN RAIN FORESTS?

The rain forests of Africa are the home of a number of Old World monkeys and other primates. There are also several forest antelopes.

The largest group of African monkeys are the guenons, such as the Diana monkey, the De Brazza monkey, Hamlyn's monkey and the moustached monkey. Each one of these has its own preferred forest layer. Other African forest monkeys include the colobus monkey and the drill, which is a ground-living baboon.

African forests also contain other primates, such as bushbabies and galagos, the potto and the angwantibo. In addition, there are apes – the chimpanzee and gorilla.

Hooved mammals are common in African forests. They include the okapi, bongo, water chevrotain, several duikers and giant forest hogs. Small mammals include elephant shrews, squirrels and scalytails. The forest hunters include the leopard, African golden cat, forest genet and slender mongoose.

▲ WHERE DO FLYING
LEMURS LIVE?

Flying lemurs, or colugos, are found in the tropical forests of South-East Asia. These forests are also inhabited by a number of primates.

The name 'flying lemur' is misleading. This animal does not actually fly, and it is no relation of the true lemurs of Madagascar. However, flying lemurs are superb gliders and can glide from tree to tree with amazing accuracy. They have features somewhere between those of bats and insectivores, and are classified in a mammal order by themselves.

Flying lemurs are not the only gliders of these forests. There are also flying squirrels, flying frogs, flying lizards and even gliding snakes.

The Asian forests are the home of the primitive tree shrews and a number of primates. These include the tiny tarsiers and the lorises. The two main groups of monkey are the langurs and the macaques, and there are two kinds of ape – the gibbon and the orang-utan.

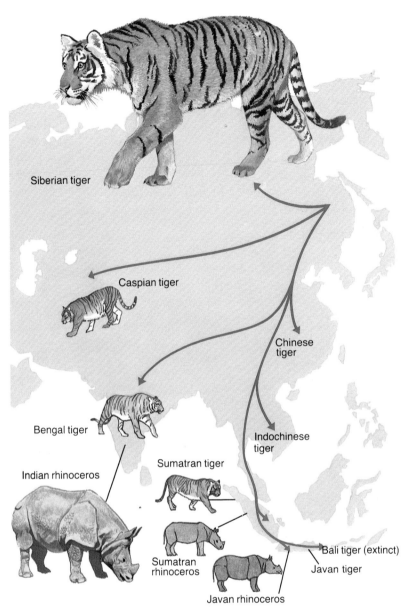

▲ WHERE DO TIGERS AND
RHINOCEROSES LIVE?

Rhinoceroses are found in Africa and South-East Asia. Tigers are found only in Asia.

Five species of rhinoceros exist today. Two of these, the black rhinoceros and the white rhinoceros, are found in Africa. Both African species have two horns.

The three one-horned species are found in India, Sumatra and Java. They are all in danger of extinction, but the most endangered is the Javan rhinoceros, which survives only in one small reserve.

The tiger is a highly adaptable animal. It originated in the cold north-east region of China. From there it spread northwards into the snowy wastes of Siberia, westwards to the Caspian Sea and southwards into the tropical rain forests of India and South-East Asia. Today naturalists recognize eight races of tiger. However, they differ only in their markings. Once all the races were widespread, but now they are all endangered.

Silvered langurs

Proboscis monkey

Mudskippers

▲ WHERE IS THE HOME OF THE ORANG-UTAN?

The orang-utan is found only in the rain forests of Sumatra and Borneo. It was once widespread throughout South-East Asia, but is now in danger of extinction because the rain forests are being cleared and young orang-utans are captured for zoos.

▲ WHERE ARE MANGROVE FORESTS FOUND?

Mangrove swamps occur where rain forest borders the sea. Mangrove forests are found in many tropical parts of the world.

Along the coasts and estuaries of tropical rain forests, the rivers deposit a rich, fine silt which forms extensive mudflats in the tidal waters. Trees and shrubs take root in the mud. The most common tree is the mangrove. Many mangroves have stilt-like roots for support. Others have special breathing roots that stick out of the mud and take in oxygen (the mud contains very little oxygen). The tangled plant life of a mangrove swamp helps to bind the mud, and in doing so gradually reclaims new land from the sea.

Mangrove forests are extensive in South-East Asia. The forests of Borneo are the home of certain langurs, such as the dusky langur, the silver leaf monkey, the strange proboscis monkey and crab-eating macaques.

The name *orang-utan* means 'man of the woods'. Like humans, individual orang-utans are easy to identify by their facial features and expressions. However, the orang-utan is less closely related to humans than the chimpanzee or gorilla.

Like the gibbons, the other Asian apes, orang-utans are tree-living animals. They can swing from branch to branch or walk along branches with great ease.

Adult males live alone for most of the time. Their huge throat pouches are used to produce loud booming sounds. Females often travel about in small groups with their young. At night an orang-utan sleeps in a rough 'nest' in a tree.

57

Little king bird
of paradise

Count Raggi's
bird of paradise

Greater bird of paradise

Red bird
of paradise

Wilson's bird
of paradise

◄ WHERE DO BIRDS OF
PARADISE LIVE?

**Birds of paradise are some of
the world's most colourful
and spectacular birds. Most
of the 43 species are found in
the forests of New Guinea.**

The ancestor of the bird of
paradise was probably a drab,
crow-like bird that made its
way to New Guinea from Asia.
Today, a few members of the
family are still rather drab, but
others are startlingly colourful.

As is the case with many
birds, it is the male bird of
paradise that is the most
splendid. Its bright colours
and long feathers are used to
attract a female mate. Display
techniques vary, enabling
females to recognize males of
their own species easily. Some
birds of paradise even display
upside down. After mating,
the females fly away to build
their nests and rear the young
on their own.

The feathers of these birds
were once much sought by
European hat-makers, and
thousands of birds were killed
each year. Today, however,
birds of paradise are protected.

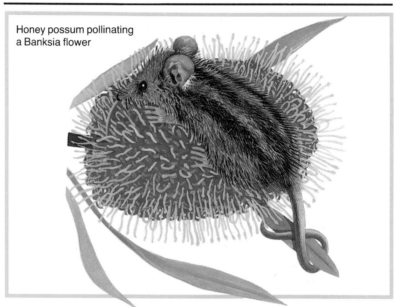

Honey possum pollinating
a Banksia flower

▲ WHERE ARE BANKSIAS
FOUND?

**The south-western corner of
Australia has a high rainfall
and luxuriant vegetation. It
is cut off from the rest of
Australia by the desert and is
the home of some unique
plants and animals. Among
these are the flowering trees
known as Banksias, and their
pollinators.**

Most brightly coloured flowers
are pollinated by insects. But
Banksia flowers are pollinated
by birds such as honeyeaters,
which visit the flowers to drink
nectar. Small marsupials such
as the honey possum also visit
these flowers. They use their
long tongues to probe deep
into the flowers. Pollen sticks
to the fur on their faces. This is
then carried to other flowers.

Other bird-pollinated plants
in this part of Australia include
certain eucalyptus trees which
are pollinated by parakeets. A
nectar-feeding parakeet has a
long tongue tipped with a
brush-like organ. The 'brush'
soaks up nectar and picks up
pollen as it is withdrawn from
the flower.

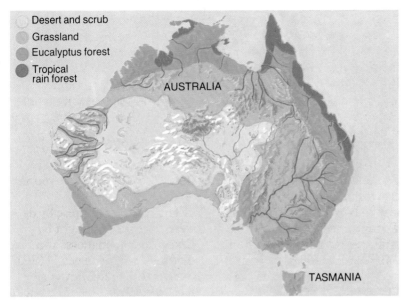

Desert and scrub
Grassland
Eucalyptus forest
Tropical rain forest

AUSTRALIA

TASMANIA

Pretty-faced wallaby

Red kangaroo

Koala

Tiger cat

Wombat

Tasmanian devil

Sugar glider

Tasmanian wolf

▲ WHAT DO MARSUPIALS EAT?

There are very few placental mammals in Australia. Instead, most Australian mammals are marsupials (pouched mammals). They occupy almost all the habitats that would normally be taken by placentals. Marsupials therefore range from peaceful grazers to fierce carnivores.

In the Americas, Europe and Asia, grassland and scrub are grazed by hooved mammals. There were no such mammals in Australia. Instead, kangaroos and wallabies became the grazers. They range from the large grey kangaroo and red kangaroo to the tiny rat kangaroo. Among this group there are also browsing forest animals, such as the tree kangaroo and the shrub wallaby.

There are no tree-living primates or rodents in Australia. Their habitats are taken by the phalangers and opossums. The cuscus, for example, is a monkey-like phalanger. Other phalangers and opossums resemble squirrels. Flying phalangers, such as the sugar glider, look exactly like flying squirrels. Most of these animals feed on plants but they also eat insects, eggs and even small birds. The koala eats the leaves of certain types of eucalyptus tree.

Rabbits and some small ground rodents have been introduced into Australia. Their marsupial equivalents, the wombat and the bandicoot, are now declining in numbers. Two other Australian ground-dwellers are the marsupial mole, which is almost identical to a placental mole, and the numbat, which is the equivalent of an anteater.

Marsupial carnivores include the dasyures, such as the tiger cat, and the eastern native cat, or quoll. These animals look more like mongooses than cats, but they are agile climbers and they stalk their prey. The so-called marsupial mice are the smallest carnivores. The largest are the Tasmanian wolf, or thylacine, and the Tasmanian devil, which eats carrion as well as live prey. Both these animals now live only in Tasmania, and the thylacine is probably extinct.

59

Himatione sanguinea

Vestiaria coccinea

Hemignathus procerus

Psittirostra cantans

▲ HOW MANY KINDS OF HAWAIIAN HONEYCREEPER ARE THERE?

On the remote islands of Hawaii honeycreepers have become even more varied than the Galapagos finches. About 23 species evolved, of which 14 still exist today.

The ancestors of the Hawaiian honeycreepers were probably finch-like birds (possibly tanagers) that managed to make the 3500-kilometre journey from North America. The honeycreepers which evolved from these travellers vary in size and colouring, but the main differences are in their feeding habits – which are indicated by the shapes of their bills.

Some honeycreepers have long, curved bills and brush-tipped tongues for drinking nectar. Others use their curved bills to probe for insects. Honeycreepers with shorter bills use them as woodpeckers do to chisel away at the bark of trees to get at insects. Seed- and fruit-eating honeycreepers have short, stout bills like those of finches.

▼ WHY ARE ISLAND ANIMALS DIFFERENT FROM OTHERS?

New species evolve in isolated places. Remote islands with stable climates provide ideal places for new species to evolve.

When a new island forms far away from any large continent, it takes time for animals to colonize it. The few animals that do arrive have to adapt to their new surroundings. For those that can adapt there are tremendous advantages.

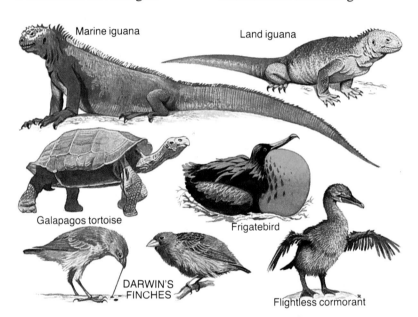

Marine iguana

Land iguana

Galapagos tortoise

Frigatebird

DARWIN'S FINCHES

Flightless cormorant

▲ WHICH ANIMALS LIVE IN THE GALAPAGOS ISLANDS?

The Galapagos Islands were formed about two million years ago. Since that time several unique species have evolved there. As well as the finches, there are giant tortoises, marine iguanas and flightless cormorants.

A Galapagos giant tortoise can measure over a metre in length. At one time each island had its own race of tortoise, but during the 1600s and 1700s visiting sailors killed them for

Unhindered by the animals that formerly preyed on them or competed with them for food, they can take over all the different types of habitat that are so freely available.

This process is called adaptive radiation and it can be seen in the finches of the Galapagos Islands. The ancestors of these finches probably flew in from South America. Over a long period of time they gave rise to the 15 different species that exist today. Each one has evolved to suit a particular type of habitat and method of feeding.

food, and some races have disappeared completely.

Iguanas probably arrived on floating logs from South America. Water and food are not as easy to find on these islands, and the iguanas adapted in two ways. Today there are land iguanas that feed on fruit and cacti and marine iguanas that feed on seaweed.

The islands provide nesting sites for a number of sea-birds. These include a flightless cormorant, the Galapagos penguin, and oceanic sea-birds such as frigatebirds and boobies.

▼ WHERE ARE MOST FLIGHTLESS BIRDS FOUND?

Flightless birds tend to live where there are few, if any, predators. A large number of flightless birds are found in Australia and New Zealand.

One of the main advantages of being able to fly is the ability to escape from predators. However, for birds that evolved in places where there were no enemies, this ability became less necessary and many abandoned flight altogether.

Unfortunately, flightless birds are extremely vulnerable to introduced predators such as cats and foxes, and to other animals such as rats, which eat their eggs and compete with them for food. Many flightless birds have also been hunted by people. Some, such as the elephant bird of Madagascar, the moa of New Zealand, many flightless island rails, and the Mauritian dodo, are now extinct.

Several flightless birds do still exist in New Zealand. The three species of kiwi are nocturnal forest-dwellers, and this has probably helped them to survive. The weka, one of the few remaining flightless rails, actually thrives on introduced animals: it eats rats and mice! On the other hand, the coot-like takahe (another member of the rail family) is in danger of extinction.

In Australia the common emu still exists in fairly large numbers, but it is the only survivor of several species of emu that lived there before the arrival of humans. Its close relatives, the cassowaries, are secretive forest-dwellers.

Emu

Cassowary

Kiwi

Weka

Takahe

► WHERE DO CRABS CLIMB TREES?

Some island animals are particularly strange and unusual. The robber crabs that live on islands in the Indian and Pacific oceans are adept tree-climbers.

Crabs are usually thought of as sea creatures, but robber crabs and other land crabs are well-adapted for living on land. Although the larvae of such crabs live in the sea, an adult robber crab will drown if left in water for more than a day.

Robber crabs are expert at climbing trees. But why they do so is something of a mystery. It was once thought that they climbed coconut palms to dislodge coconuts, which they then cracked open and ate. However, a robber crab is quite unable to get inside a coconut. And, in fact, its main food is carrion: dead animal matter that is washed up on beaches. They do eat the flesh of coconuts, but only after the coconuts have been broken into by other animals. They also eat certain fruits.

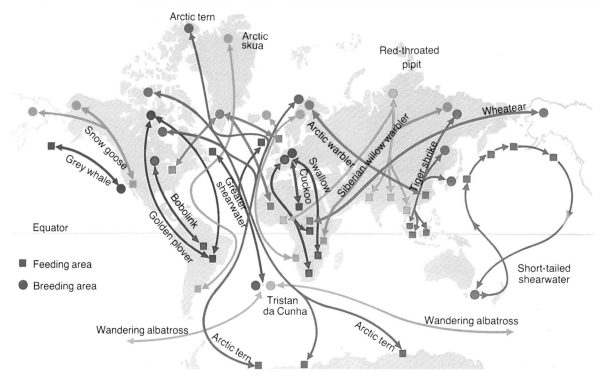

Arctic tern

Arctic skua

Red-throated pipit

Snow goose

Grey whale

Wheatear

Arctic warbler

Siberian willow warbler

Tiger shrike

Swallow

Cuckoo

Greater shearwater

Bobolink

Golden plover

Equator

■ Feeding area

● Breeding area

Tristan da Cunha

Short-tailed shearwater

Wandering albatross

Arctic tern

Arctic tern

Wandering albatross

▲ WHY DO BIRDS MIGRATE?

A migrating bird typically moves from a summer breeding area to a winter feeding area. The reasons for such migrations include the availability of food and avoiding extreme cold.

The migrations of northern birds may have started at the end of the last Ice Age. As the ice cap melted, some birds moved north in summer to take advantage of the food that became available. Each winter they retreated south again, but gradually their journeys became longer and longer.

The most northerly birds migrate south to avoid the Arctic winter. The Arctic tern covers the longest distance: it migrates all the way to the Antarctic. Farther south, the migratory birds are mostly insect-eaters that cannot find enough food in winter. Seed-eaters and omnivorous birds often remain in the same area all year.

▲ WHERE DO SHEARWATERS MIGRATE TO?

Shearwaters, or petrels, are sea-birds that breed in large colonies in the same place each year. Outside the breeding season some shearwaters make long journeys.

The Manx shearwater breeds only on certain European coasts. But during the remaining months of the year it wanders around the Atlantic Ocean. The greater shearwater breeds on the island of Tristan da Cunha between November and April, but spends July and August in the North Atlantic.

Between October and March, short-tailed shearwaters breed in thousands off the coasts of Tasmania and south-eastern Australia. But in April they begin a complete circuit of the Pacific Ocean. This migration enables them to take advantage of the abundant fish supplies of the North Pacific Ocean.

▲ WHY DO WHALES MIGRATE?

Most migratory animals breed in their northern range. But northern whales migrate south to breed in warmer waters. Southern whales migrate in the opposite direction.

The best-known whale migration is that of the California grey whale. This animal feeds all summer in the Bering Sea. Its autumn migration route follows the coast of North America to breeding lagoons off the coast of California.

Other migrating whales include the blue whale and the humpback whale. There are populations of these whales in both the northern and southern hemispheres. The northern populations move south to summer breeding grounds, and the southern populations move north. But because the seasons of the two hemispheres are different, the two populations never meet.

▼ WHERE DO MONARCH BUTTERFLIES MIGRATE TO?

The two main populations of monarch butterflies are found in North and South America. Both populations move nearer to the Equator in the autumn.

Most butterflies migrate to some extent, but monarchs make longer journeys than most. They may fly 3000 kilometres to their winter feeding areas.

In summer the North American population of monarchs is spread across southern Canada and the northern USA. In autumn they gather in groups and move south until the whole population reaches the southern part of North America. There they spend the winter in huge clusters.

In spring they mate and begin to move north again. But the adults that set out are not those that eventually reach Canada. Two or three generations may pass before the population is once again back in its northern area.

▼ WHERE DO GREEN TURTLES LAY THEIR EGGS?

Like all sea turtles, green turtles lay their eggs on land. They spend the rest of their time at sea, but each year they return to the same beaches to lay their eggs.

Green turtles are found in tropical and subtropical waters all round the world. They were once very numerous, but they have been hunted by people for their flesh. Today, there are only about a dozen major nesting beaches left. These beaches are usually on islands. A green turtle may travel as far as 2000 kilometres to reach its own nesting beach.

On reaching the beach, a female waits until night. Then she crawls out, digs a nest and lays about 100 eggs which she covers with sand. About eight weeks later the eggs hatch and the young wait near the surface for a few days. Then, during the night, they emerge and head for the sea. Many are eaten by predators such as crabs, cats, sea-birds and sharks.

▼ WHERE DO EELS BREED?

Eels live in fresh water and migrate to the sea to lay their eggs. They breed only in the Sargasso Sea.

When female eels are between 7 and 12 years old (4-8 years old in the case of males) they leave their inland rivers and head downstream to the Atlantic Ocean. They spawn in the Sargasso Sea.

The adults die and the larvae hatch out. As they drift away from the Sargasso Sea, they grow. By the time they reach the rivers they have changed into adults.

The European and American eels are usually thought of as being two different species, but in fact there is little difference between them. If they are different species, how do the young larvae sort themselves out as they leave the Sargasso Sea? One idea is that adult eels from Europe do not in fact ever reach the breeding area, and that both the European and American eels come from eggs laid by American eels.

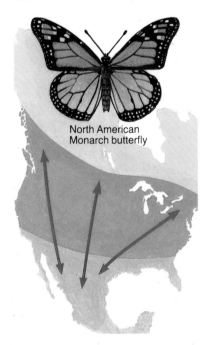

North American Monarch butterfly

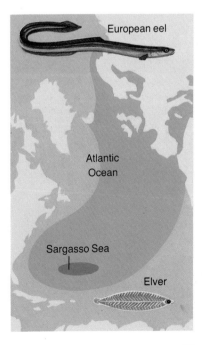

European eel

Atlantic Ocean

Sargasso Sea

Elver

THE PAST

**Almost four million years
ago, creatures very like
ourselves walked the Earth.
We know this because they
left their footprints behind.**

At Olduvai Gorge in Tanzania,
East Africa, scientists have
unearthed some of the oldest
known human remains. They
found bones, stone tools, and
even signs of a crude stone
shelter.

At nearby Laetoli, an even
more amazing find was three
sets of footprints, preserved in
a layer of volcanic ash. They
show that three people (two
adults and a child) passed that
way about 3,700,000 years ago.
The footprints provide one of
the earliest clues to the puzzle
of when the first true humans
appeared on Earth.

**We do not know exactly
where people first
discovered how to grow
plants for food. It was
somewhere in the Middle
East, about 9000 years ago,
and it probably happened in
a fertile river valley.**

Before people became farmers,
they had to gather fruit and
berries or hunt animals for
food. Farming began when
people started to harvest wild
wheat and oats. But it was a
much bigger step to gather
seeds, clear the ground and
plant fields.

Instead of wandering, the
first farmers had to stay in one
place to tend their crops. They
gave up hunting and, instead,
kept herds of animals such as
sheep, goats, pigs and cattle.

Farming was the beginning
of civilization. Trade grew as
farmers sold food to their
neighbours. And, by cutting
down trees and clearing the
land to make fields, human
beings began to change the
appearance of the Earth.

▼ WHERE WERE WHEELED CARTS FIRST USED?

In history, a few inventions have altered the course of civilization. Perhaps the most important of all engineering inventions was the wheel.

The wheel appears to have been invented in several parts of the Near East and Asia at roughly the same time – around 3000 BC. Perhaps the potter's wheel existed before the cart-wheel.

Primitive people used sledges to drag loads. Someone must have thought of putting wooden rollers (such as tree branches) underneath the sledge. This made it easier to pull. Fitting an axle, with wheels at each end, was a much more difficult step.

The first wheels were probably cut from tree trunks. They were solid and clumsy. Wheels with spokes came later, about 2000 BC.

To make full use of the wheel, an animal is needed to pull a cart. The first carts were pulled by people, but in time animals were trained for this work.

▼ WHERE DID PEOPLE FIRST USE WRITING?

Stone-Age people 'wrote' in pictures. In time, pictures were turned into 'picture-signs'. This was the beginning of writing.

About 6000 years ago, people in Babylon, China and Egypt had learned to use picture-signs. They made marks in wet clay with their fingers or with sticks. A picture of the Sun, for example, might mean 'heat'.

Later, people invented signs that stood for sounds or ideas, rather than pictures. The Sumerians, for example, used a cuneiform, or wedge-shaped, script. A stick was used for writing the marks on clay tablets. Some of the earliest written records are sums or tally marks made by clerks to keep count of goods or animals.

Around 1500 BC, the Phoenicians invented an alphabet based on sounds. From this come the alphabets we use today.

▼ WHERE WAS PAPER FIRST MADE?

Paper is the most common material used today for writing and printing on. It was unknown in ancient times until the Chinese invented a method of paper-making.

In ancient Egypt, people wrote on papyrus-reed scrolls. In Babylonia, they made marks on tablets of wet clay. The Romans wrote on sheets of parchment (very thin leather).

In about AD 100, the Chinese found out how to make thin sheets of paper from pulped fibres and rags. They kept the secret to themselves for hundreds of years.

Later, the Arabs discovered the secret and, much later, the art of paper-making spread to Europe. By the 1300s there were paper mills in France, Spain, Italy and Germany.

The invention of printing machines in the 1450s led to a great increase in the use of paper. Without paper, the rapid increase in book-production, and the spread of knowledge that went with it, could not have taken place.

◄ WHERE WAS SILK FIRST PRODUCED?

Silk was first made in China. Threads from silkworm cocoons were spun on spinning wheels, then woven into fine cloth.

The Chinese found out how to make silk over 5000 years ago. They guarded the secret, for silk was a rare fabric and very costly. Traders made the long journey along the 'Silk Road' to buy Chinese silk, travelling from as far as India and the Middle East.

In AD 552 two Persian monks smuggled the secret of silk-making out of China. They hid silkworm eggs inside hollow bamboo canes, and also took seeds of the mulberry tree, whose leaves silkworms eat.

In time, people in Europe learned how to rear silkworms (the larvae of the silk moth) and to make silk. Silk was used to make fine, soft robes for rulers and nobles. To make silk, the delicate thread used by the silkworm to spin its cocoon must be unwound. As much as 300 metres may be unwound from one cocoon.

► WHERE WAS THE POTTER'S WHEEL INVENTED?

Pottery was one of the earliest inventions. At first, pots were shaped by hand out of wet clay. Turning pots on a wheel came later.

The wheel was invented in Sumeria, Babylon and elsewhere in the Near East around 3000 BC. Clay pots had already been made for over 5000 years, but they were crude and often broke.

Making pots is a skilful craft. The potter needs skill not only in spinning the wheel to shape the pot, but also in firing the pot in a kiln to harden it. The first potters learned also how to glaze (coat) pots with various substances to make the pots stronger and more decorative.

The invention of the potter's wheel led to one of the first industries – pottery. A skilful potter could make enough pots to exchange them for food and other goods, or sell them for money.

◄ WHERE WERE THE FIRST OLYMPIC GAMES HELD?

Every four years, from 776 BC, the Greeks held a great festival. Artists, writers and athletes gathered to honour the great god Zeus. The contests were held at Olympia, and became known as the Olympic Games.

The first Olympic Games were not just sporting contests. There were plays and recitals by poets, as well as races. To the Greeks, the Games expressed the union of mind and body, striving for victory to honour Zeus, the king of the gods.

The events lasted for three days. Athletes ran, wrestled, rode horses and drove chariots. The Games began with the Olympic oath and ended with prizes and feasting.

The Olympic Games continued until AD 393. They were then forgotten until 1896, when they were revived at Athens on the suggestion of a Frenchman, Baron Pierre de Coubertin. They continue to be held every four years.

▶ WHERE DID THE GREEKS FOUND COLONIES?

The rulers of ancient Greece encouraged people to set off and found new colonies overseas. So Greek civilization spread far beyond its birthplace.

By the 8th century BC, Greece could no longer feed its growing population. The rulers of the Greek city-states feared discontent. So they were happy to see some of their citizens leave home to found new Greek colonies, where there was land for all.

Some Greek colonists went east to the Black Sea. But most journeyed west to Italy, Sicily and southern France. A few went as far as Africa, including Egypt.

Each Greek colony became a 'little Greece' in a strange land. The Greek settlers traded for goods with the cities where they had once lived. In this way Greek skills and Greek ideas were carried to new cities all around the Mediterranean coast.

◀ WHEN DID PEOPLE FIRST USE MONEY?

Today we use money to buy things. But when trade began thousands of years ago, there was no money. So people exchanged goods. The invention of money made trade much simpler.

The first metal coins were minted (made) in about 800 BC. Before then, all trade had been done by barter – that is, by exchanging goods. For example, a tool-maker might barter tools in exchange for meat or clothing.

As civilization developed, trade became more complex. Barter was a clumsy method. A trader needed small, easily-carried tokens to exchange, but the tokens had to be valuable. So the first coins were made of metal, in particular gold and silver.

Gold coins have real value. Paper money, on the other hand, is merely a token. The paper itself is worthless. Paper money was invented in China, and was in use there by AD 800.

▶ WHERE WERE ROADS FIRST PAVED?

When people first began to travel, they followed rough tracks and trails. In bad weather, it was safer to stay at home. Paved roads were not thought of until wheeled carts came into use.

The earliest paved roads were made in Babylon some 4000 years ago. As people began living in towns and trading with their neighbours, they needed better transport. A cart could not cross wild country, for fear of breaking an axle or sinking into mud or sand.

Many ancient cities had paved roads, and we can still see their remains today. But undoubtedly the greatest road-builders of the past were the Romans. Their roads ran straight from town to town.

Roman roads were built by army engineers. They were made of stones and gravel, and cambered (sloped) so that rain would drain away to the sides. Roman armies marched swiftly along these fine roads to keep the peace within the Roman Empire.

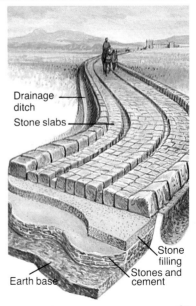

Drainage ditch
Stone slabs
Stone filling
Stones and cement
Earth base

▼ WHERE WAS THE PLOUGH INVENTED?

The first farmers tilled the soil with hand ploughs rather like garden hoes. It was in Mesopotamia, around 4000 BC, that farmers began using oxen to pull ploughs.

The plough was probably invented before the wheel. It began as a rough wooden tool, dragged up and down a field to scratch the surface of the soil. The farmer sowed seeds in the channel made by the plough.

Around 500 BC, a much improved plough appeared. It had a blade, or share, tipped with iron. And it was made in such a way that the blade turned the soil completely over, making a furrow.

In the Middle East, a small plough worked perfectly well. But larger ploughs were needed to tackle the heavy, hilly soils of northern Europe. Some ploughs were so heavy that they needed a team of up to eight oxen to pull them. Because the oxen could not turn sharply, fields became very large. Each field was divided into long strips, with drainage ditches in between.

▼ WHERE WERE ANIMALS FIRST USED FOR FARM WORK?

The first farmers worked with their hands, using simple tools. Training animals to pull ploughs and carts, as well as work machines, made the farmer's life much easier.

An ox is much stronger than a human. It can pull a heavier plough, and do more work in a day. The use of oxen to help with farm work dates from about 4000 BC in Mesopotamia, in the 'fertile crescent' where farming began.

The animals that could be tamed in this way were herd animals such as cattle, asses, horses and camels. Oxen were harnessed with a wooden yoke across their necks. The yoke was not suitable for horses, however, and so horses were kept only for riding until much later, when the horse-collar harness was invented.

In the Middle East, animals were used to provide the power for simple machines, such as water pumps for irrigating fields. Animals were used everywhere to carry loads.

▼ WHERE DID THE FIRST KEY TURN IN A LOCK?

Once people had more than just one or two possessions, they needed a way of keeping property safe. The earliest locks were made in Egypt in about 2000 BC. They were clumsy, but they worked.

The locks invented by the ancient Egyptians were made of wood. The idea was simple. A door was kept shut by a bolt slid across the door and into a slot in the door frame. The bolt had several holes drilled in

it. When it was slid shut, pins in the lock dropped down into the holes. The bolt was then held fast.

To open the lock, the pins had to be lifted free. This was done with a key which was pushed into a hole in the bolt. Only the right key, with the right number of pegs cut into it, would fit.

The Egyptians took great trouble to secure the rich tombs of the pharaohs against thieves. Even so, many tombs were plundered and stripped of their treasures.

68

▼ WHERE WAS IRON FIRST SMELTED?

Iron must be heated in a furnace before it can be shaped to make tools. The secret of 'smelting' iron was discovered in the Near East around 1500 BC.

As early as 4000 BC, people had learned to make tools and weapons from copper, which is a fairly soft metal. Copper can be hammered into shape when cold. In Sumeria, smiths found that copper and tin could be mixed to make bronze.

Iron is much stronger than copper or bronze. To smelt it, a very hot furnace is required. Ancient iron tools have been found at Ur of the Chaldees and inside Egyptian tombs. By 1200 BC iron had replaced copper and bronze.

Iron was thought to be magical, and the smiths who forged iron swords and spears were believed to have supernatural power. The Greeks valued iron as highly as gold. The Chinese, who invented efficient bellows to make furnaces very hot, made fine iron.

▼ WHERE WERE IRON WEAPONS FIRST USED IN WAR?

War in ancient times was fought at close range. But then, as now, the 'arms race' was on. The first soldiers to use iron weapons were the Assyrians. They became the most feared of all.

The first real armies were those of Assyria and Egypt, some 3000 years ago. Before then, wars were fought mainly by small groups of warriors. Egypt had many soldiers, but few wore any kind of protective clothing. Egyptian archers used reed arrows tipped with stone or copper.

Iron, the new metal, was harder and sharper. The Assyrians discovered how to use it in warfare. They made iron heads for their spears and arrows. For defence, the Assyrian soldiers wore long coats of iron chain-mail.

Iron weapons were much stronger than weapons made of copper or bronze. Sword, spear, shield and armour could be made of iron, making the 'iron warrior' much more formidable than his foes.

▼ WHERE WERE THE FIRST ROCKETS FIRED?

The Chinese invented the rocket. From this simple firework have come today's space rockets and missiles.

The first rockets were tubes filled with gunpowder (a mixture of potassium nitrate, charcoal and sulphur). The Chinese discovered thousands of years ago that gunpowder explodes when burned. Packed into a tube, the exploding gunpowder pushed out a stream of hot gas, sending the tube flying off in the opposite direction.

The Chinese let off fireworks for fun, but also fired rockets as weapons of war. In the Middle Ages, the invention spread to Europe. During the wars of the early 1800s the British army used rocket batteries to bombard Copenhagen in 1807 and during the battle of Leipzig in 1813.

The forerunner of the modern long-range rocket was the German V2. This was used during World War II.

69

▼ WHERE DID HOUSES
FIRST HAVE CENTRAL
HEATING?

Until the 20th century, most people in cold countries kept warm beside open fires. We think of central heating as a modern invention. In fact, the Romans had central heating 2000 years ago.

The Romans were excellent builders. Their houses had proper drains and their towns had good water supplies. A wealthy Roman's house usually had underfloor heating too.

The heat came from a furnace. The floor was built on brick pillars so that hot air from the furnace could flow freely beneath it and up through pipes to rooms above. This system was known as a hypocaust. At the public baths, the hypocaust heated water for the hot pools and steam rooms. There Romans would meet to relax and enjoy a bath, and maybe a massage.

The Romans built central-heating systems throughout their Empire. But after the Romans, the secret of the hypocaust was forgotten.

▼ WHERE DID ALEXANDER
LEAD HIS ARMY?

Alexander, King of Macedonia, was a famous warrior. He was called 'the Great' because he led his army to victory after victory.

Alexander was born in 356 BC. Macedonia was then a small kingdom in Greece. Becoming king at the age of 20, Alexander set out on an astonishing quest for power.

First, he conquered the other city-states of Greece. Then he took on the mighty

▲ WHERE DID THE ROMANS
BUILD HUGE AQUEDUCTS?

An aqueduct is a bridge or channel built to carry drinking water into a city. The Romans built aqueducts so well that some still exist today.

Every Roman town needed a reliable water supply. Sometimes it was necessary to build an aqueduct to bring water from a nearby lake or river. The aqueduct was either a conduit (channel) or a huge bridge carrying a canal on top.

Persian Empire and defeated it. He invaded Egypt and founded the city of Alexandria.

Even then, his ambition was not satisfied. He led his army into India, but his troops were weary of conquest. They refused to march further, and Alexander had to turn back.

In 12 years, Alexander was never defeated. He was only 33 when he died. After his death, his vast empire broke up. After Alexander, no other general could rule such a conquest.

Near Nîmes in France is an aqueduct built by the Roman general Agrippa. It has three storeys, or tiers, raised on arches. The longest aqueduct was over 85 kilometres long. One of the most famous was called the Aqua Appia. It was built in 312 BC to carry water into Rome, and was over 16 kilometres long. Nearby ran the road called the Via Appia, or Appian Way. Both were built by the Roman military engineer Appius Claudius Caecus.

WHERE DID THE ROMAN EMPIRE END?

The Roman Empire was the greatest of ancient times. Rome's rule stretched from Britain in the west to the Black Sea in the east. Its Empire lasted for 500 years.

Rome began as a small kingdom in what is now Italy. The Romans first conquered Italy (by 200 BC), then the other Mediterranean lands and North Africa. They eventually ruled most of western and central Europe.

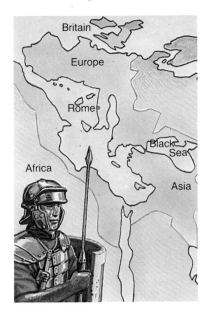

Augustus became the first Roman emperor in 27 BC. Roman rule brought peace to the conquered lands. But the Roman armies were faced with attacks from barbarians living beyond the Empire.

In AD 476 the barbarians captured Rome. By then the Empire was weak and divided. Only in the East, with its capital at Constantinople, did the Roman Empire survive. The Eastern Empire lasted until Constantinople fell to the Turks in 1453.

WHERE WERE THE FIRST UNIVERSITIES FOUNDED?

A university is a place of 'all learning'. New knowledge in the Middle Ages led to the setting up of great centres of learning throughout Europe. Many of these universities are still in existence today.

By the 1300s, knowledge was growing rapidly. For centuries education had been left to the Church. Now, all over Europe, universities came into being.

Great universities were founded in cities such as Paris, Bologna, Oxford, Cambridge and Prague. The only subjects taught at first were law, theology (religion) and medicine. One of the first medical schools was founded in the 9th century at the university of Salerno in Italy.

Each university was granted a royal charter. This gave it privileges and the right to award degrees to its students. Scholars from all over Europe taught at the universities. They taught in Latin, the 'universal language'. Today there are universities in many countries, teaching a variety of subjects.

WHERE HAS THE MOST ANCIENT BIBLE BEEN FOUND?

In 1947 a goatherd came across some ancient scrolls in a cave close to the Dead Sea. These scrolls contain parts of the Bible written perhaps 200 years before the birth of Christ.

The Dead Sea Scrolls caused great interest among scholars. Reading and preserving the scrolls required much patience and careful work. The scrolls had been rolled inside jars for

safe-keeping, and they had to be unrolled with great care.

Almost every book of the Old Testament appears, at least in fragments, in the scrolls. The oldest passages from the Book of Leviticus, were written in an early Canaanite form of Hebrew.

The scrolls were probably stored in the caves by Jews at the time when Palestine was ruled by Rome. The hot, dry desert air helped to preserve the fragile scrolls. From them we have learned much about how the Bible came to be written.

► WHERE DID MUHAMMAD FLEE?

The religion of Islam was founded by the Prophet Muhammad. In AD 622 he had to flee from his home in Mecca to Medina.

Muhammad was born in about AD 570 in Mecca, in present-day Saudi Arabia. At the age of 40 he set out to call people to a belief in one God.

Muhammad was persecuted when he began preaching. With a few followers, he was forced to flee from Mecca to Medina. His flight is known as the Hegira, and the Islamic calendar is dated from it. For some years there was war between the Meccans and the followers of Muhammad. In 630, Muhammad captured Mecca.

The words of God, as revealed to Muhammad, were written down in the Koran, and the religion he founded grew to be one of the great faiths. To Muslims (followers of Islam), Mecca and Medina are holy places.

► WHICH EUROPEAN CITY WAS THE CAPITAL OF AN ISLAMIC EMPIRE?

The Moors were a Muslim people of North Africa. They created a large empire, which included part of Spain, and made Seville their capital. The Moors took Islamic art, science and learning to Europe.

The Moors originally lived on the Barbary coast of North Africa. They were converted to Islam in AD 707. At this time Islam was growing fast, and the Moors took part in this expansion.

They invaded Spain, and remained powerful there for hundreds of years. They made Seville, their capital city, a centre of Islamic culture. Islamic civilization was more advanced than that of medieval Europe, especially in the fields of science and medicine.

Christian leaders fought against the Moors. Gradually, the power of the Moors weakened. In 1238 they retired to Granada, the last Moorish kingdom in Europe, and were eventually driven out in 1492.

◄ WHERE WAS CATHAY?

Before the 13th century, Europeans knew little of Asia. To them, Cathay (China) was an unknown land. No Europeans had been there until the Polo family made their journeys.

Chinese civilization was the oldest on Earth, but the Chinese cared little about the world outside. In Europe, only a few fantastic stories of 'Cathay' were known.

In 1260, the brothers Niccolo and Maffeo Polo set out from Venice to trade in the East. They returned in 1269 with tales of their visit to Cathay, where they had met its Mongol ruler, Kublai Khan.

In 1271 they left Venice once more. With them went Niccolo's son, Marco. The overland journey to China took four years. The Polos did not return to Venice until 1295. Marco travelled throughout China in the service of Kublai Khan. When he returned, Marco wrote a book about his travels. From it, Europeans discovered that they had much to learn from the Chinese.

For people in medieval Europe, winter was a hard time. There was little food for farm animals, so most were killed in autumn. **Spices were used to preserve and flavour meat during the winter. These spices came from Asia.**

The need to disguise the bad taste of rotten meat led Europeans to explore the oceans. This is strange, but true, for the spices the Europeans needed came from the Spice Islands, in what are now the East Indies.

The journey overland was long, with the result that spices were very costly. In the 1400s, Europeans searched for new sea routes to the Indies.

When Columbus landed in the New World in 1492, he hoped he had reached the Spice Islands. He was wrong. But the quest for spices had led to the discovery of a vast new continent.

The Chinese were the first people to print books on paper. They used wood blocks for this. Much later, the mechanical printing press was invented.

The earliest known printed book was made around AD 868. It is called the *Diamond Sutra* and was hand-printed, using wooden blocks. This printing method is slow. Even so, it is faster than copying books by hand. In Europe, at that time, all books were copied by hand – usually by monks. Books were so precious that they were often chained to reading stands.

In the 1400s, a German known as Johannes Gutenberg invented a printing machine. This used separate pieces of metal type for each letter. The letters were arranged in order to make up a whole page of words. This was then printed by a screw-type press. The printing press made it possible to print books in much larger numbers.

In the Middle Ages, the longbow was the main 'long-range' weapon. Often it was the archers who decided the outcome of a battle.

In 1337, England and France went to war. The war lasted more than a hundred years. In 1346, the English army won the battle of Crécy. The English success owed much to their skill with the longbow. In 1415, English and Welsh archers won another battle, at Agincourt.

The longbow was powerful and accurate. With it, an archer could bring down a knight on horseback. The longbow could be shot more rapidly than its rival, the crossbow. Medieval kings encouraged archery as a sport, to ensure that there would be a ready supply of trained bowmen for use in war.

Archers were also carried on warships. Many longbows have been found in the wreck of the English ship *Mary Rose*, which sank in 1545.

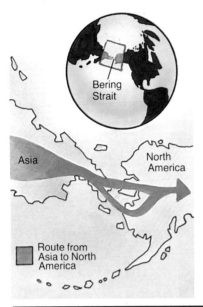

◀ WHERE DID THE AMERICAN INDIANS COME FROM?

When Columbus discovered America he thought he had reached the Indies, in Asia. So he called the people 'Indians'. Columbus was wrong. But the American Indians had in fact come from Asia thousands of years earlier.

The American Indians look rather like the Mongols who still live in eastern Asia. The Indians crossed a 'land bridge' to reach North America. Today, the two continents are separated by a channel of sea called the Bering Strait.

The Indians began settling in America about 25,000 years ago. They lived by hunting and farming. There were many groups, or tribes, and each had its own customs and beliefs.

The Indians had to travel on foot, since the horses which had once lived in America had died out before the Indians arrived. It was the Spanish who re-introduced horses to America in the 1500s.

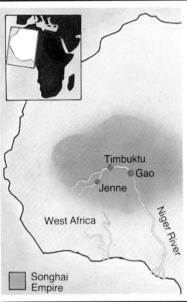

◀ WHERE WAS THE SONGHAI EMPIRE?

In the 1500s there was a rich and powerful empire in West Africa. This was the empire of the Songhai, who were soldiers, farmers and traders.

The Songhai Empire included lands in the countries we now call Mali, Niger and Nigeria. The Songhai people controlled the trade and fishing along the great Niger River. From around AD 800, they played an important part in West African events. The Songhai kings challenged the Islamic rulers of the Mali Empire farther north. For many years there was war.

The Songhai grew rich on the salt and gold trades. They controlled the caravan routes to the north. Their downfall came in the late 1500s. Already weakened by squabbles between its princes, Songhai was attacked by Moroccan armies. The Moroccans had firearms and, with the help of these new weapons, captured the important Songhai towns of Gao and Timbuktu.

◀ WHERE WAS EL DORADO SUPPOSED TO BE?

El Dorado is Spanish for 'the golden one'. Early explorers in South America heard strange tales of a land so rich that its ruler bathed in gold dust.

We now use the expression 'El Dorado' to mean an imaginary country full of riches. But the tales the early Spanish adventurers heard, as they explored South America in the 1500s, told of a man, not just a country.

El Dorado was said to be the chief of a tribe living in a marvellous city called Omoa. Each year, as part of a great sacred festival, the chief bathed in gold dust, for the land was so rich that gold was as plentiful as water.

El Dorado was supposed to live somewhere in what is now Colombia. None of the Spanish explorers who went in search of his fabulous land ever discovered it. But they did find plenty of gold elsewhere in South America.

► WHERE DID THE PILGRIM FATHERS LAND?

In November, 1620, a small ship landed in North America. It was called the *Mayflower*. On board were some 35 settlers from England, remembered today as the Pilgrim Fathers.

The Europe from which the Pilgrim Fathers came was torn by religious quarrels. The Pilgrim Fathers wanted peace to set up a Church of their own, so they decided to risk the perilous two-month voyage across the ocean to America.

The Pilgrim Fathers planned to sail in two ships. But when one proved unsafe, all the passengers crowded aboard the *Mayflower*. The sea voyage was stormy but they reached America and settled where Plymouth, Massachusetts, now stands.

Half of the settlers died during the first winter. But the colony survived to harvest its first crops in November 1621. This is remembered in the USA today as Thanksgiving Day, on 24 November.

► WHERE DID A TEA PARTY START A REVOLUTION?

The colonists of America were tired of old ways. They wanted to govern themselves. When Britain tried to tax its colonies in America, the colonists protested. The American Revolution followed.

By the mid 1700s there were 13 British colonies in America. The colonies made their own local laws but the British government kept control of money and trade.

In 1763, the British also gained control of French territory in North America. To raise money for stationing troops there, the British government tried to tax the colonists. One of the taxes was on tea.

The Americans protested. In 1773 a group of colonists crept on to a ship in Boston harbour. Disguised as Indians, they threw its cargo of tea into the water. The 'Boston Tea Party' began a revolution, leading to American independence in 1783.

► WHERE DID THE OPIUM WAR BREAK OUT?

The war of 1840-42 between Great Britain and China is called the Opium War. It started when the Chinese government tried to stop Europeans from importing the illegal drug opium into China.

For hundreds of years China had tried to keep out foreign traders, but Europeans were eager to profit from the trade in opium, a drug which was smoked in pipes.

The Chinese government tried to end this trade, and destroyed the British merchants' stocks of opium. The British declared war and attacked China.

The Opium War ended in 1842 with the Treaty of Nanking. This opened five ports in China to British trade, and handed over Hong Kong to Britain. China was also forced to pay damages to the British merchants.

This began a period of foreign domination of China, which was to be the cause of the later Boxer Rebellion.

▶ WHERE DID AMERICAN SLAVES FOUND A FREE COUNTRY?

During the 1700s many Africans were taken to work as slaves in America. In 1822 a homeland for freed slaves was set up in Africa. Its name was Liberia.

In America, rich white people owned many black slaves. But others fought to end the evil of slavery. This struggle eventually led to the US Civil War (1861-65).

A few black slaves won their freedom before the Civil War, but they were homeless. They decided to return to Africa, the land from which their ancestors had been taken in the slave ships.

Liberia, the land of freedom, was founded in 1822. Its capital, Monrovia, was named after the US President James Monroe.

Today, Liberia is an independent republic. Many of its citizens can trace their ancestry back to those first settlers who made the return journey from America to Africa.

◀ WHERE DID THE BOXER REBELLION TAKE PLACE?

In the 1890s powerful European countries controlled much of China's trade. The Chinese uprising against this unfair control is known as the Boxer Rebellion.

The 'Boxers' were members of a patriotic secret society called the 'Society of the Righteous and Harmonious Fists'. They were angered to see China falling more and more under foreign influence. In 1900 the Boxers rose in rebellion to drive out the foreigners. The Empress Dowager, Tzu-hsi, encouraged the rebels.

In the capital, Peking, the Europeans took refuge inside their embassies. The siege of Peking lasted 55 days before an international army fought its way into the city to rescue the Europeans.

After the Boxer Rebellion, the Europeans demanded that China pay compensation. The Boxers had failed; but they had shown how weak the Chinese emperors had become. In 1911 China became a republic.

▶ WHERE DID TANKS FIRST PLAY A PART IN WARFARE?

World War I was a war of terrible machines. Trench warfare killed thousands of soldiers. In 1916 a strange new weapon crawled into battle – the tank.

The generals could not understand the new warfare. As whole armies became bogged down in the muddy trenches of Europe's battlefields, they looked for a breakthrough. Cavalry had been made out of date by barbed wire and machine guns. A new weapon was needed.

In the summer of 1916, during the battle of the Somme, the British introduced the first tanks. They were armoured tractors, crawling on caterpillar tracks, firing cannon and machine guns. Not even a trench could halt them. They were sent into battle singly, to help soldiers on foot. Only a few people saw that the tank's future lay in mass onslaughts. This was proved in World War II when German tank armies swept across much of Europe in a few weeks.

◀ WHERE DID THE LEAGUE OF NATIONS MEET?

After the slaughter of World War I, many nations sought a lasting peace. The League of Nations was set up in 1920 with the aim of settling quarrels peacefully. The League met at Geneva, in Switzerland, but it was doomed to fail.

The League of Nations was meant to act as a world council, but it had no real powers. The leader who did the most to bring the League into existence was Woodrow Wilson, the President of the USA. Unfortunately, Wilson could not persuade the USA to join the League. Other states, such as Germany, left the League as soon as their own behaviour was criticized.

The League could not prevent the world slipping into another war in 1939. It had failed. In 1945, the United Nations Organization was set up, with similar aims. The UN has been more successful, but still lacks the power to be a true 'world government'.

▶ WHERE WERE THE FIRST ATOMIC BOMBS DROPPED?

World War II was nearly over by 1945, but Japan fought on. To end the war, a terrible new weapon was used: the atomic bomb.

During World War II, both sides worked to make an atomic bomb. Scientists from many countries gathered in the United States. There the first atom bomb was tested on 16 July, 1945.

By 1945, Germany was defeated but Japan was still fighting. To land armies in Japan would have been slow and costly. So the Allies decided to use their new weapon. On 6 August, 1945, an atomic bomb was dropped on the Japanese city of Hiroshima. On 9 August, a second bomb was dropped on Nagasaki.

Both cities were destroyed. Over 100,000 people were killed and an equal number were injured. The war was over, but the world now feared the terrible destructive power of the atomic bomb.

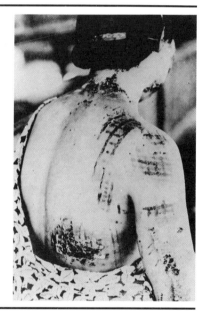

◀ WHERE WAS THE SIX-DAY WAR FOUGHT?

The state of Israel came into being in 1948. Since then, Israel has fought several wars with neighbouring Arab countries. In 1967, the Israelis won a war in just six days.

Israel was founded in what had been Palestine. The Jews had long dreamed of a homeland, a reborn Israel. But the Arabs living in Palestine and neighbouring states opposed this idea.

After World War II, many Jewish people went to live in Palestine. The homeland was declared and in 1948 the state of Israel came into existence. At once there was war between Israel and its neighbours.

Israel has fought many wars since 1948. In 1967, Israel fought both Egypt and Jordan. The Israeli armies, helped by air attacks, won a rapid victory in six days. Israel captured the west bank of the River Jordan and seized much Egyptian territory in Gaza and Sinai.

PEOPLE AND PLACES

▼ WHERE DO PEOPLE LIVE IN TENTS?

Most tent-dwellers are nomads of West and Central Asia. Nomads need homes that they can move from place to place because they have to wander with their flocks and herds to find fresh pastures.

Famous tent-dwelling nomads include the Bedouin of Arabia. These desert-dwellers live in long, low tents that are made of black goats'-hair cloth held up by poles and ropes pegged in the sand. One strip of cloth serves as the roof. Another strip protects one side from the wind. Bedouin tents are light to carry and easy to erect.

The Kazaks and Mongolians of Central Asia use another kind of tent – the *ger* or *yurt*. Yurts look more like portable huts than tents. They consist of thick layers of felt laid over a wooden frame, with an outer covering of hide or canvas. Strong and gale-proof, yurts keep out the bitterly cold winds that sweep across Central Asia in winter.

▼ WHERE DO PEOPLE LIVE IN WOODEN HOUSES?

Wooden houses are found mostly in areas where there is plenty of timber, for example North America, northern Europe and the Far East.

In Europe people build wooden houses among the mountains of lands such as Austria, Germany, Switzerland, Norway and Sweden. Mountain chalets are made of pine or fir logs. These have heavy timbers and broad overhanging roofs.

European settlers took their building skills to North America. They made log cabins roofed with bark, thatch or wooden tiles called shingles. Today many American and Canadian homes have a timber frame and outer walls made of overlapping wooden planks.

Bedouin tent

Mongolian yurts

▼ WHERE DO PEOPLE LIVE IN HOUSES ON STILTS?

There are several parts of the world where you might see houses built on stilts. These are where people have raised homes over shallow water, or on land likely to be flooded.

Many stilt houses stand in shallow, sheltered coastal waters in South-East Asia or on Pacific Ocean islands. Strong, long wooden posts (piles), driven deep down into mud, form a firm foundation for these buildings.

Fishing villages of pile dwellings rise from lagoons in the Philippine Islands. These homes have wooden floors and walls, and steep, thatched roofs. People build other kinds of wooden-framed pile dwellings on Polynesian islands, in New Guinea, along the Amazon River, and on lagoons in West African countries such as Benin.

Stilt houses have been built for thousands of years. In Italy and Switzerland there are remains of pile dwellings which stood on the shores of lakes in Bronze-Age times.

▼ WHERE DO PEOPLE LIVE IN MUD HOUSES?

People build mud houses mostly in lands where mud is a more plentiful material than wood or stone, and where there is hot sunshine to bake the soft mud hard.

Many African peoples build huts with walls made of mud. In the Sudan, some Nuba families each have a cluster of five round mud huts with thatched roofs. One hut serves as a bedroom, another is a barn, and so on. In northern Nigeria people build mud houses that have straight walls and a flat roof.

Unusual mud homes outside Africa include the beehive-shaped mud houses built by Arabs in the Syrian Desert. In Mexico and the south-west of the United States there are so-called adobe houses. These are made from mud that has been mixed with straw, and then shaped into bricks and left in the sun to dry.

Few houses are built of mud in climates that are wet or cold. Rain and frost would soon wash away the mud or make it crumble into dust.

▼ WHERE DO PEOPLE LIVE ON BOATS?

In the Western world some people live on barges and flat-bottomed boats called houseboats. But most of the world's boat-dwellers live in East Asia on craft that are much smaller.

Most boat-dwellers live in China, Japan and nearby islands. Many Chinese people spend their lives on boats moored just off the overcrowded island of Hong Kong. Where there is no space to build a home on land, or the land is too expensive, thousands of families have no choice but to live on water.

In Hong Kong harbour and the big Chinese rivers, most boat-dwellers live on light craft called sampans. A sampan usually has a small cabin with a roof made of mats. Inside, a whole family will cook, eat, work and sleep.

Life is cramped. Sometimes it is dangerous as well. Tropical storms and huge waves set off by earthquakes can sink sampans moored in shallow seas, or drive boats ashore.

◄ WHERE CAN STONE-AGE PEOPLE STILL BE FOUND?

Some peoples still live an almost Stone-Age way of life in several of the world's wild places. These include Africa's Kalahari Desert, the Amazon Forest of Brazil and the island of New Guinea. But the most primitive people of all are the Tasaday of Mindanao, an island in the Philippines.

Scientists first visited the Tasaday in 1971. They found 25 Tasaday people living in a cave halfway up a wooded hill. The Tasaday make and use stone tools and fire, but their only clothes are leaves. They eat crabs, fish and tadpoles. The Tasaday catch these by feeling for them under rocks in mountain streams. They also collect and cook wild plants.

The Tasaday are peaceful people and get on well together. There is no single leader of the group. One scientist thought they were the gentlest people on Earth. Perhaps our early Stone-Age ancestors led lives much like those of the Tasaday.

► WHERE DO THE MASAI LIVE?

The Masai are a group of African cattle-keeping people. They live east of Lake Victoria in the highlands of Kenya and Tanzania.

The Equator crosses Masai territory from east to west, and the Great Rift Valley runs from north to south.

Masai are tall and slim with a high, narrow head and slender hands and feet. Most live in villages of mud-and-brushwood huts set in a circle. Family groups consist of a man, his wives and their children. Young men become warriors and live in separate villages.

Most Masai eat mainly maize and millet, but warriors feed on milk and blood. They obtain blood by cutting a vein in the neck of a cow or bullock. The cut later heals. Masai also kill sheep for food, but eat cattle only if these die of injury or illness. Warriors with spears and shields guard the herds. They may also raid the cattle of their neighbours.

◄ WHERE DO BUSHMEN LIVE?

Bushmen live in the Kalahari Desert, a barren part of south-west Africa. Some still hunt and gather food, as all people used to in the Old Stone Age.

The ancestors of Bushmen lived in much of southern Africa until they were driven out by other Africans. Today the Bushmen live in the Kalahari Desert, an open waste with little water and few trees.

Bushmen are small, slight people with yellow-brown skin and tightly curled hair. They keep no animals and grow no crops, but they are skilful hunters. Bushmen imitate the cries of wild beasts to lure their prey nearer. They kill antelope with bows and arrows, and set snares for smaller beasts.

Women gather edible insects, roots and berries. Bushmen know how to find juicy bulbs and how to use a reed to suck up moisture from wet sand. They can survive where most people would quickly die of thirst or hunger.

► WHERE DO SHERPAS LIVE?

Sherpas are a group of hardy people who live in Nepal, a kingdom north of India among the towering Himalaya Mountains.

Sherpas live in the Khumba Valley of north-east Nepal, close to the world's highest peak, Mount Everest. They grow grain and potatoes and keep sheep and cattle.

Sherpas are a sturdy people related to the Tibetans farther north. Many belong to the Buddhist faith. They are well known as the hard-working porters who carry loads for mountain-climbers in the Himalayas. Sherpas can carry immensely heavy loads on their backs all day. What is more, they can work at heights where most people would feel dizzy and faint.

The most famous of all the Sherpas is Tenzing Norgay. With the New Zealand climber, Edmund Hillary, Tenzing Norgay became one of the first two people to reach the top of Mount Everest, in June 1953.

◄ WHERE DO THE AINU LIVE?

The Ainu are a people who live on certain islands in the north-west Pacific Ocean. Most live in Japan, but they do not closely resemble other Japanese people.

Some Ainu inhabit remote parts of Japan's large northern island, Hokkaido. Others live nearby on the Kurile Islands and Sakhalin Island in the Soviet Union. Many live in fishing villages.

In certain ways, the Ainu seem to resemble people of European rather than Japanese ancestry. Their bodies are heavily built and covered with much hair. Also, their hair is brown, not black like the hair of most of the peoples of East Asia. Some experts think that the Ainu are descended from an ancient group that once lived in much of Asia.

The Ainu had their own language, lived by fishing and hunting, and worshipped spirits. They wore clothes of skin or bark-cloth. But their old customs are now disappearing.

► WHERE DO GYPSIES COME FROM?

Gypsies are a wandering people found in many parts of the world. Their English name is short for 'Egyptian', but the gypsies' true home was probably India.

Many experts believe that gypsy travellers wandered west from India about six hundred years ago. They went through Iran and reached Syria and Egypt. By the 1500s some had reached Europe. Many entered Romania, Hungary, Russia, France, Spain and England. A few even crossed the sea to North America.

Thousands of gypsies still spend their lives wandering. They live in caravans and find work as traders, metalworkers or musicians. Some work in fairs; others deal in horses or used cars.

Gypsies tend to have dark skin, dark wavy hair, and big black or brown eyes. Many speak Romany, a language that comes from an ancient Indian tongue. Gypsies enjoy dancing and singing. They keep to their old traditions.

▶ WHERE DO ABORIGINES LIVE?

Aborigines are a country's earliest inhabitants. The best-known aborigines are those of Australia.

Australian Aborigines have dark-brown skin and wavy hair. Their ancestors may have migrated from South-East Asia about 40,000 years ago.

Aborigines lived in small wandering bands and made simple shelters at resting places. They used weapons and tools made from wood and stone to hunt and gather food. One of their weapons was the boomerang. This is a throwing weapon made from wood. One type is cleverly designed to return to the thrower.

Australian Aborigines had their own music, art and religion. At times they would gather for a corroboree, a festival of music and dancing.

There were about 300,000 Aborigines in Australia when Europeans first arrived there two hundred years ago. Many Aborigines were persecuted by European settlers, and now only about 110,000 remain.

◀ WHERE DO MAORIS LIVE?

The Maoris are the native people of New Zealand. Indeed the word *Maori* means 'native'.

Maoris mostly have light-brown skin, brown or black hair and eyes, a broad face with high cheekbones, and a straight nose. They tend to be tall and strongly built.

Maoris speak a Polynesian language. Hundreds of years ago their ancestors sailed from far-off Pacific islands in huge canoes. They were the first people to discover and settle in New Zealand.

When British settlers arrived in the early 1800s, Maoris were Stone-Age farmers, hunters and fishermen. They were skilled carvers, tattooists and weavers, and sang songs and war chants.

Maoris could be fierce warriors. At times their tribes fought British settlers. But later both groups made peace and intermarried. Maoris now lead a modern way of life but they keep up their customs. The Maoris shown here are wearing traditional dress.

▶ WHERE DO THE TUAREG LIVE?

The Tuareg are nomads of northern Africa. Some roam the Sahara Desert. Others live on its southern edge.

The Tuareg belong to the Berber peoples, who lived in North Africa long before the Arabs arrived. They speak the old Tuareg language and use an ancient kind of writing. The Tuareg are Muslims. In contrast to many Muslims, the Tuareg men, not the women, veil their faces.

There are two Tuareg classes: nobles and vassals. Nobles own camels, goats, sheep and farms set in oases. Vassals mind the nobles' livestock. Negro serfs grow crops on the nobles' farms.

Tuareg are independent and proud. They once raided and traded far across the Sahara. They also fought against the French Foreign Legion. But many Tuareg have now left the desert to find more fertile land to the south. Their old ways of life are vanishing fast.

◄ WHERE DO PYGMIES LIVE?

Pygmies are very small people, mostly living a primitive life. Groups live in remote parts of Africa, the Andaman Islands of the Indian Ocean, Malaysia and the Philippines. Their numbers are few and becoming fewer still.

The best-known pygmies are the African pygmies, known as Negrillos. These live in the hot, steamy forests of Central Africa. Negrillos look very like small Negroes. A full-grown Negrillo is no taller than a 10-year-old Negro boy of normal height.

African pygmies gather wild plants, catch fish, and use poisoned arrows to shoot animals such as monkeys and antelopes. They do not grow crops or keep farm animals.

Negrillos wear few clothes, but make bags and pottery and build simple huts. They are wanderers, but each small group has its own territory. Negrillos trade meat for iron tools and food grown by Negro tribes in the forest.

► WHERE DO ESKIMOS LIVE?

Eskimos live in the cold polar regions of North America and north-east Asia. They are related to the Chinese and Japanese. Their ancestors probably migrated across the Arctic thousands of years ago.

Eskimos are well built to survive long cold, Arctic winters. Their short, stocky bodies store heat better than those of tall, thin people.

Eskimos have learnt how to cope with the cold. They make warm fur coats and build turf-roofed homes, half hidden underground. In winter, hunters far out on the ice build snow houses called igloos.

Eskimos are skilled at fishing and hunting seals and whales. Their hunting boats are slim, skin-covered canoes called *kayaks*. On land, teams of dogs haul sleds that carry equipment and dead game. But old ways of life are dying. Many Eskimos now live in wooden houses in towns.

◄ WHERE DO LAPPS LIVE?

Lapps live mostly in the region of northern Europe called Lapland. This covers parts of northern Sweden, Finland, and the USSR.

Lapps are short, strongly built people. They have straight black hair, low foreheads, and high cheek bones. Many have flat noses and thin lips. Lapps have their own language. They wear colourful clothes of wool and reindeer skins.

Different groups live in different places. Mountain Lapps lead a wandering life with their reindeer herds. Each family shares one tent.

River Lapps live a more settled life along river banks. Besides reindeer, they keep cattle and sheep. River Lapps hunt and fish, and some grow a few crops. Sea Lapps live in wood and turf huts built on the coast. Most work as fishermen.

The Lapps' ancestors lived in Central Asia. They reached Lapland thousands of years ago. Some Lapps now move out of Lapland and marry people to the south.

When the High Dam was built at Aswan on the River Nile, a great lake formed behind it. To prevent the water engulfing them, two temples at Abu Simbel were dismantled and rebuilt on higher ground.

The Egyptian Pharaoh Ramses II had the temples built at Abu Simbel about 3200 years ago. They were carved out of the face of a cliff beside the River Nile. The Great Temple had 14 rooms and stretched 60 metres into the cliff. Four huge stone seated figures of Ramses II flanked the entrance. Six huge figures guarded the other temple.

In the 1960s, the new Aswan High Dam blocked the Nile and its waters rose. To save the temples, workmen cut them into huge blocks weighing 20 to 30 tonnes each. They raised these to the nearby hilltop, then fitted them together again. About 50 nations gave money to pay for this colossal project.

This is a narrow rocky gorge in southern Egypt. Ancient Egyptians buried many of their kings in the valley.

The Valley of the Kings lies on the west bank of the River Nile, near the ancient Egyptian city of Thebes. Here, in the desert, people have discovered more than 60 tombs. They were made more than 3200 years ago.

Each tomb consists of corridors and rooms cut deep into solid rock. Sculptors and artists carved and painted religious signs and writing on the walls. When a king died, people laid his body here inside a great stone coffin. They also left rich treasures for his use in an after-life.

Tombs had secret doors and deep pits to keep out robbers. In time, though, thieves plundered almost every tomb. Only one tomb remained intact. It belonged to Tutankhamun, a young, unimportant king, yet its splendour astonished the archaeologists who found it.

The biggest ancient Roman amphitheatre is the Colosseum in Rome, Italy. Amphitheatres were early sports stadiums. They had a central arena surrounded by seats. Indeed, their name means 'theatre on both sides'.

The remains of the Colosseum still stand, near the centre of Rome. Its outer walls are 49 metres high, and it measures 187 metres in length and 157 metres in width.

More than 86,000 spectators could sit or stand on tiers raised on arches. They looked down on a big oval central arena. Engineers could flood this for šea-battles. But the Romans used it mostly for fights to the death between trained fighters called gladiators, or between people and wild animals.

The Romans built the Colosseum by AD 80. Its name came later from a colossus (a huge statue) of the Emperor Nero. The Emperor Hadrian had this placed at the entrance.

▶ WHERE WERE PYRAMIDS DISCOVERED IN THE JUNGLE?

Since the late 1700s, explorers have found many ancient ruined pyramids in the forests of Central America. American Indians had built the pyramids centuries earlier.

Old stone pyramids stand in parts of Mexico, Belize, Guatemala, El Salvador and Honduras. They were used as temples. Most had flights of steps that led up to a small room on top. Here, priests used to sacrifice animals or people to their gods.

The first of these pyramids were built more than 3000 years ago. Some are the largest (but not the tallest) pyramids on Earth. Pyramid-builders included peoples such as the Zapotecs, Mixtecs, Mayas, Toltecs and Aztecs.

In time, the pyramids and nearby towns were abandoned. This probably happened when the land around no longer produced enough crops or water to meet the needs of the people.

▶ WHERE IS THE LOST CITY OF THE INCAS?

The lost city of the Incas is Machu Picchu in the Andes Mountains of Peru. It is called 'lost' because the Incas abandoned it, and the city remained unknown to explorers for several centuries.

Machu Picchu stands only 80 kilometres north-west of the city of Cuzco. But it is perched on a narrow mountain ridge about 2060 metres above sea level. Forests hide it from below. This is why it stayed forgotten until the American explorer Hiram Bingham rediscovered it in 1911. Bingham found houses, temples, and a hundred stairways. All were built of huge, well-fitting blocks of uncemented stone.

Bingham named the ruins Machu Picchu ('Old Peak') after a nearby mountain. But the Inca name seems to have been Vilcabamba. In 1580, the last Inca ruler of Peru may have fled to Machu Picchu to escape the Spanish who had seized the Inca Empire.

▶ WHERE IS ANGKOR WAT?

Angkor Wat is a great temple which was built by the Khmer people of South-East Asia. It lies in Kampuchea, a country also known as Cambodia.

Angkor Wat means 'city temple'. This temple is the largest religious building in the world. Its outer wall encloses an area larger than a dozen full-sized soccer pitches.

Inside stand several stone enclosures, each taller than the one outside it. In the middle rise five huge stone towers shaped like lotus flowers. Sheets of beaten gold once covered them. The middle tower is tallest, so the whole temple is shaped rather like a vast pyramid. Carvings on the walls of corridors show scenes from stories about Vishnu, a Hindu god.

A Khmer king, Suryavarman II, had Angkor Wat built in the early AD 1100s. Later, it was abandoned. A Frenchman, Henri Mouhot, discovered the overgrown ruins in the early 1860s.

Jerusalem is a holy city for people who belong to the religions of Judaism, Christianity and Islam. Jerusalem was once split between Jordan and Israel. In 1967 Israel seized all of it.

People of different faiths consider Jerusalem holy for different reasons. For the Jews, it was their ancient Hebrew capital, where King Solomon built the Temple. For Christians, the city is important because Jesus preached and died there.

Muslims believe that the Prophet Muhammad rose to heaven from a rock in Jerusalem. A beautiful shrine, known as the Dome of the Rock, now stands over the rock.

The Western (Wailing) Wall is especially holy to the Jews. Many Christians believe that the Church of the Holy Sepulchre marks the place where Jesus was buried. The picture shows the Dome of the Rock and the Wailing Wall in front of it. Jews gather at the Wall to pray.

The Wailing Wall, or Western Wall, is a high wall in eastern Jerusalem. It is one of the oldest, holiest places in Jewish history.

Today the wall forms part of the boundary of a Muslim sanctuary which includes the Dome of the Rock. The wall's proper name is the Western Wall. Some of it seems to be the remains of the western part of a far older wall. This surrounded the great Temple founded by King Solomon nearly 3000 years ago. The Temple has been destroyed and rebuilt several times. The Romans destroyed the last Temple in AD 70.

The Wailing Wall is about 49 metres long and about 12 metres high. Its huge blocks of stone are built up in 28 layers. Only the lowest probably date back to the time of Solomon. Jews pray at the wall. They bewail the fall of the Temple and other disasters that befell their people long ago. They also pray to God for help in the future.

The Roman Catholic Church has its centre at Vatican City, in Italy's capital, Rome. The Vatican Palace is the home of the Pope, the head of the Roman Catholic Church.

The Pope reigns from Rome because Roman Catholics believe that St Peter made Rome the centre of the early Christian Church. Catholics believe that Christ chose Peter to be the head of the Church on Earth. They think of St Peter as the first bishop of Rome, and the popes as St Peter's successors.

St Peter is thought to lie buried in the Vatican, under St Peter's Basilica (shown here). This is the world's largest church. It is built in the shape of a cross and crowned by a vast dome. Beneath this, a huge bronze canopy covers the altar. St Peter's can hold up to 50,000 people. Huge crowds gather outside, in the immense Square of St Peter, to hear the Pope speak from a balcony.

▲ WHERE IS THE HOLY CITY OF THE HINDUS?

The Hindus' holy city is Varanasi in India. It stands on the River Ganges in the north-central state of Uttar Pradesh. It used to be known as Benares.

Varanasi stands on the left bank of the Ganges, in south-east Uttar Pradesh. To Hindus, this city is one of the holiest places on Earth. They believe that worshipping their gods at the river brings a special reward. They also believe that dying there will free them from having to be reborn.

More than a million pilgrims go to Varanasi each year from all over India. They wade into the Ganges at the *ghats*, bathing places where steps lead down to the river.

Pilgrims worship in the city's 1500 temples. Rows of temples, shrines and palaces rise from the bank of the Ganges. Many have beautifully carved decorations. For Hindus the most important building is the Golden Temple, which honours the god Shiva.

▼ WHERE DO CHRISTIANS MAKE PILGRIMAGE?

A pilgrimage is a journey to a holy place, or shrine. The greatest Christian centre of pilgrimage is at Lourdes in south-west France.

Lourdes is a town in the region of Hautes-Pyrénées, near the Pyrenees Mountains. Roman Catholics believe that the Virgin Mary appeared there several times in 1858 to a peasant girl. Fourteen-year-old Bernadette Soubirous said she had seen these visions in a cave at nearby Massabielle. In 1862, the Roman Catholic Church declared it believed the visions had taken place.

More than two million pilgrims from all over the world now visit Lourdes each year. Many are very ill. They hope to be cured by spring waters in the cave which are said to have healing powers.

In 1958 an immense underground church, the Basilica of St Pious X, was built at Lourdes. It can hold up to 20,000 pilgrims at once, and is the second largest Roman Catholic church in the world.

▼ WHERE IS THE BIGGEST STATUE OF BUDDHA?

The largest statue of Buddha stands near the town of Bamian. This is in the north of Afghanistan, a country of west-central Asia between Iran, Pakistan and the USSR.

Bamian lies in the valley of the Bamian River. This is about 2600 metres above sea level, in the Hindu Kush Mountains west of the Himalayas.

About 14 centuries ago, Buddhist monks cut hundreds of cave-dwellings into the soft cliffs lining the valley north of the town.

Bamian became famous as a centre of Buddhist worship and art. Sculptors carved two huge statues of Buddha out of the solid rock. They added on ridges of mortar to look like the folds in clothing. The larger figure stands 53.3 metres high and once gleamed with jewels and gold.

Also near Bamian are the remains of the world's longest statue, over 300 metres long. Built of rubble covered with plaster, it shows Buddha lying down.

▲ WHICH CITIES ARE BUILT ON CANALS?

Venice and Amsterdam are canal cities. Venice, shown here, is built on islands divided by canals. Amsterdam stands on land below sea level and is drained by canals.

Venice lies in north-east Italy, in the Adriatic Sea. It was founded in AD 452 by people escaping from barbarian invaders of mainland Italy. Venice later became a rich trading city, and many great palaces and churches were built on its islands.

Venice has more than 1500 canals crossed by over 400 bridges. Many of the houses stand on wooden posts sunk in the mud. The islands are now sinking, and many of the buildings have been damaged by rising water.

Amsterdam is the capital of the Netherlands. It was founded in about 1275 and became a great trading centre in the 1500s. The city stands on low-lying land and is drained by a network of canals shaped rather like a spider's web.

▼ WHERE ARE THE LOW COUNTRIES?

The Low Countries are the Netherlands, Belgium and Luxembourg. They lie in north-west Europe and are bordered by France, West Germany and the North Sea. They are known as the Low Countries because much of their land is low-lying.

The Netherlands is the most low-lying of the Low Countries (its name means 'Low Lands'). About 40 per cent of its land has been reclaimed from the sea. These areas, known as polders, are below sea level and are surrounded by dykes. Machines continuously pump water out of the polders into drainage ditches and canals. Windmills were once used for this.

Belgium lies south of the Netherlands. Its northern region, Flanders, consists of low-lying polders. But the Ardennes, in the south-east, is a hilly forested region. Luxembourg, to the south-east of Belgium, also has hills and lowland. It is one of the smallest countries in Europe.

▶ WHERE IS THE BLACK FOREST?

The Black Forest is a mountainous region in the south of West Germany. It borders the River Rhine, in the province of Baden-Württemberg.

The Black Forest measures about 160 kilometres from north to south, and varies between 16 and 40 kilometres in width. The northern part is mostly a sandstone plateau, and there are granite mountains in the south. The highest point is a peak called the Feldberg. This is 1500 metres above sea level. The River Danube begins in the Black Forest.

Dark forests of firs and spruces cover the mountains in much of the north. These give the Black Forest its name. Oak

and beech forests grow on the slopes, and grapes and other fruits are grown in the valleys.

Tourists visit the Black Forest for hiking holidays. Many stay at local towns such as Baden-Baden, which have mineral springs.

▼ WHERE IS VERSAILLES?

The city of Versailles is in northern France, a few kilometres south-west of Paris. Nearby stands the palace of Versailles.

The palace of Versailles was built for King Louis XIV in the late 1600s. Before then, Versailles consisted of a few houses in woods where the French kings went hunting.

The palace is more than 800 metres long and has hundreds of rooms. Many of the rooms are splendidly decorated. The

palace overlooks a huge park with lawns and walks laid out in patterns. There are pools and fountains also, and a canal which is 1.6 kilometres long. Drives lead through the park to two smaller palaces called the Grand Trianon and the Petit Trianon.

Several historic events have taken place at Versailles. A meeting of the French parliament there in 1789 led to the start of the French Revolution. In 1919 the Treaty of Versailles, marking the end of World War I, was signed in the palace.

▼ WHERE ARE GOTHIC CATHEDRALS FOUND?

Many cathedrals were built in the Gothic style in Europe between the 1100s and 1400s. The earliest and finest of these are found in northern Europe.

Gothic cathedrals are tall, graceful buildings with pointed arches and slender pillars. Many have brightly-coloured stained-glass windows. Early critics of this style of architecture named it after barbarian tribes called the Goths.

The earliest Gothic cathedral was built at Sens in northern France. One of the most splendid is Chartres Cathedral (shown here), also in northern France. This was built between 1194 and 1225.

Chartres Cathedral has the widest nave and the tallest spires in France. Its great stained-glass windows show saints and scenes from the Bible. It also has a maze through which worshippers used to crawl on their knees. The cathedral stands on a hill and its tall twin spires can be seen from a great distance.

▼ WHERE IS TROOPING THE COLOUR HELD?

Trooping the Colour is a ceremony held in London. It takes place each year on the British monarch's official birthday.

Trooping the Colour takes place on Horse Guards Parade on a Saturday early in June. The ceremony involves carrying a regimental flag, or Colour, between formations of soldiers. Each year a different regiment's flag is trooped, but the regiment is always one of those in the Household Brigade of Guards. These form the sovereign's personal bodyguard, and the sovereign acts as each regiment's colonel-in-chief.

First, the guards line up along two sides of a square. Then the brigade's massed bands form up. A sergeant with two guardsmen bears the Colour to the front of the parade. All three salute the sovereign, who then inspects the parade. Trooping the Colour follows. Colours used to be carried on to the battlefield to identify each regiment.

▼ WHERE IS THE PONTE VECCHIO?

Ponte Vecchio means 'old bridge'. The Ponte Vecchio is the oldest and most famous bridge in Florence, the capital of Tuscany in Italy.

The Ponte Vecchio stands on the River Arno which flows through the city. The bridge is many hundreds of years old and was rebuilt in 1345.

Unlike modern bridges, the Ponte Vecchio has a row of buildings containing shops along each side of it. The backs of these goldsmiths' and jewellers' shops jut over the river on wooden brackets. Instead of shops, three open arches flank each side of the middle of the bridge.

Long ago, a corridor was built on top of the bridge to connect the Pitti Palace south of the river with the Uffizi Palace which stands on the north bank. The corridor was damaged in World War II. The Ponte Vecchio was the only bridge in Florence which was not destroyed in World War II.

▲ WHERE IS THE ESCORIAL?

The Escorial stands in central Spain, about 50 kilometres north-west of Madrid. It is a huge building with several parts, including a church, a convent, a palace and a royal burial place.

The Escorial rises among the Guadarrama Mountains as a great grey granite rectangle with towers at the corners. It has 86 stairs, 1200 doors and over 2600 windows. There are also 1600 paintings and a big library.

The Escorial is one of the finest Spanish buildings put up in the late 1500s. From the outside it looks grim, but there are splendid rooms and courtyards inside. The best features include a great domed church and a cloister with a fountain.

King Philip II had the Escorial built as somewhere to live, pray and study quietly, and as a royal tomb. Philip II and some of Spain's later kings were buried under the church.

▼ WHERE IS THE LEANING TOWER?

The Leaning Tower is in Pisa, a city of Tuscany in west-central Italy. Some people rank the tower as one of the wonders of the modern world. It began tilting hundreds of years ago.

The Leaning Tower is the bell tower of the cathedral of Pisa. It stands 54.5 metres high and measures 15.8 metres round the base. The top of the tower is over four metres out of line with the base. It leans so far that it looks as if it will topple over at any moment.

Construction of the tower began in 1174 but it remained incomplete until 1350. Before it was half finished, the ground sank under its weight and the tower started tilting. Since 1918, yearly measurements have been made. They show that the lean is increasing.

The tower is made of marble and built in a style known as Romanesque. Rows of rounded arches resting on columns surround its eight floors. People can climb to the top of the tower by a stairway inside.

▼ WHERE IS THE
ALHAMBRA?

**The Alhambra is a famous
old palace fortress at
Granada, a city in southern
Spain. It was built by the
Moors, a Muslim people
who ruled Spain in the
Middle Ages.**

The Alhambra stands on a hill
below the Sierra Nevada
mountains and overlooking
Granada. The Moorish kings
of Granada built the Alhambra
between 1248 and 1354. It was
the last Moorish stronghold in
Europe. Its name is Arabic for
'the red' and probably comes
from the red bricks of its outer
wall.

The wall and its 13 towers
enclose the palace and gardens.
The palace is small but lovely.
Slim columns, marble floors,
tiled walls and lace-like
mouldings on walls and
ceilings adorn its chambers
and courtyards. Mouldings
show words from the *Koran*,
the holy book of Islam,
delicately done in Arabic
script. Fountains play from
pools in the courts and
gardens. Palms and other subtropical plants grow there.

▲ WHERE IS THE KREMLIN?

**The Kremlin is the old
centre of Moscow, the
capital of the Soviet Union.
Its walls and towers rise
from a hill on the left bank of
the River Moskva.**

The name *kremlin* comes from
a Russian word meaning
'fortress'. The Kremlin is a
group of buildings surrounded
by high walls crowned with 20
towers and entered through six
gates. The walls form a
triangle with sides that total
2.4 kilometres in length.

The first walls were built of
wood, eight centuries ago.
Today's great walls date from
the late 1400s. Inside, splendid
cathedrals with gilded domes
face a central square. Here,
too, is the Great Kremlin
Palace.

The Kremlin was once the
Russian emperor's Moscow
home. Now the Soviet
government and the
Communist Party hold
meetings there. The Kremlin
has many art treasures and
since 1955 it has been a
national museum.

▲ WHERE IS RED SQUARE?

**Red Square lies just outside
the north-east wall of the
Kremlin in Moscow. Its
name comes from an old
Russian word that means
'red' or 'beautiful'.**

Red Square is an immensely
broad, paved open-space about
400 metres long. It forms the
most famous of the so-called
central squares in the heart of
Moscow.

Red Square is best-known
for the huge parades that pass
through to celebrate May Day
and the anniversary of the
Russian Revolution.
Thousands of people march
past in processions that last
several hours. Russian leaders
watch from above the Lenin
Mausoleum.

The photograph shows Red
Square and the wall of the
Kremlin. In front of the
Kremlin is Lenin's tomb.
Every day, Russians visit the
tomb to pay homage to Lenin,
the founder of the modern
Soviet Union. In the
background is St Basil's
Cathedral, with its cluster of
colourful domes.

◄ WHICH GREAT CITY HAS HAD FOUR NAMES?

Istanbul, in north-west Turkey, was once called Constantinople or New Rome. Earlier still, people called it Byzantium.

Istanbul is Turkey's largest city and seaport, and one of the world's oldest cities. Part stands in Europe and part in Asia. Separating both parts lies a narrow strait called the Bosporus, which links the Black Sea with the Mediterranean.

According to legend, a Greek called Byzas founded Byzantium on the European side of the Bosporus in 657 BC. In AD 330, the Emperor Constantine made Byzantium the capital of the Eastern Roman Empire. Constantine enlarged it and renamed it New Rome, but it became known as Constantinople (from Greek words meaning 'Constantine's city').

In 1453, the Turks captured Constantinople. It became known as *Istanbul*, a Turkish version of Greek words meaning 'in the city'.

◄ WHERE IS THE KRAK DES CHEVALIERS?

This huge medieval castle stands in the mountains of Western Syria. It was one of the greatest castles to be built in the 12th century.

The Krak des Chevaliers, or Krak of the Knights, began as a fort called the *Hisn el-Akrad*: 'Castle of the Kurds'. Christian Crusaders seized it from their Muslim enemies in 1109, and then rebuilt it. Using forts in the East as a model, they made an outer 'curtain wall' protecting an inner stronghold, with tall linked towers.

The Krak's defenders could stand at slits in the top of the outer wall and its towers to fire arrows or hurl stones at attackers below. From holes in the wall, they could pour hot pitch on to their enemies' heads.

The Krak was one of the most important castles for defending the borders of the states set up by Christian Crusaders. The Knights Hospitallers held it from 1142 to 1271.

◄ WHICH ARE THE RICHEST COUNTRIES IN THE WORLD?

This depends on how you measure a country's wealth. One way is to work out the wealth of each person in a country, supposing that all the wealth were shared out equally. Measured in this way, the wealthiest countries are a few Arab states in south-west Asia.

The richest Arab states are those with small populations but huge supplies of valuable oil. Profits from the sale of oil have helped such states to improve their standard of living. Most of these states are on the Persian Gulf.

The states with the most wealth per head of population in the early 1980s were the United Arab Emirates. Altogether these had fewer than one million people. If all wealth were shared equally among their people, in 1980 each person would have had 30,070 US dollars.

The photograph shows an oil rig on the Persian Gulf. Excess gas from the oil is being burned off.

► WHERE IS ISFAHAN?

Isfahan stands in western Iran, about 400 kilometres south of the capital, Tehran. Isfahan is an old city with some splendid buildings.

Isfahan's name may come from an Old Persian word for 'army camp' but the city grew up as a trading centre set in rich farmlands watered by the Zaindeh ('life-giving') river.

In 1598, Shah Abbas the Great made Isfahan the Persian capital. The Shah rebuilt it as one of the world's largest and loveliest cities. He added the huge Royal Square, palaces, public buildings and mosques. Many of these still exist.

The photograph shows the Masjid-i-Shah (Royal Mosque) at the south end of the Royal Square. The mosque's dome is covered in blue enamelled tiles that shine brilliantly in sunlight.

West of the Royal Square stands the Ali Qapu ('lofty gate'). This archway, crowned by a high covered balcony, leads into the gardens of the old royal palace.

► WHERE IS BANGLADESH?

Bangladesh is a small Muslim country in tropical Asia. It is almost surrounded by eastern India which lies along its western, northern and eastern borders. On its southern boundary is the Bay of Bengal.

The name Bangladesh means 'Bengal nation'. Bangladesh stands on the Bay of Bengal where the great delta of the Ganges and Brahmaputra rivers juts into the sea.

Bangladesh is less than two-thirds the size of the United Kingdom, yet its population is almost twice as big. Farmers grow rice and other tropical crops on rich soil in the hot river plain and delta. Bangladesh produces most of the world's jute, a plant that yields fibres used for making sacks and wrappings.

When India and Pakistan became independent in 1947, Bangladesh became part of Pakistan, and was known as East Pakistan. After a war in 1971, Bangladesh became a separate country.

► WHERE IS THE GATEWAY OF INDIA?

The Gateway of India is a great archway on the waterfront of the port of Bombay, in western India.

India's British rulers built the Gateway to mark a royal event. This was a visit to India in 1911 by King George V and Queen Mary. At that time, the British sovereign was also the emperor of India.

Its architect built the Gateway of India as a kind of mighty triumphal arch, a type of building made famous long before by the Romans. But he designed its arches and towers in the Indian Gujarat style of the 16th century.

It seemed fitting to erect the Gateway of India in Bombay. Under the British, this port on the Arabian Sea had grown into the main port of arrival for ships sailing to India from Europe and North America. Its deep-water harbour, protected by islands, has helped to make Bombay one of Asia's great cities.

◄ WHERE IS THE TAJ MAHAL?

This beautiful tomb stands in a garden outside the city of Agra, in north-central India. The Mogul Emperor Shah Jahan had the Taj Mahal built in memory of his favourite wife, Mumtaz Mahal.

Shah Jahan ordered work to begin after his wife died in 1631. Some 20,000 workmen spent more than 20 years making the tomb and laying out its garden.

The bodies of Shah Jahan and his wife lie in a vault below a tall, eight-sided building of white marble, pierced by immense arches and crowned by a delicate dome. This mausoleum stands on the middle of a great square marble platform. Four tall prayer towers, or minarets, rise from its corners.

Two identical mosques of marble and red sandstone flank the mausoleum. The group of buildings stands in a walled garden, where a long pool reflects the domed mausoleum.

► WHERE IS THE GOLDEN PAGODA?

The Golden Pagoda is a great Buddhist shrine which overlooks Rangoon, the capital of Burma. Its proper name is the Shwe Dagon Pagoda.

The Shwe Dagon Pagoda rises 112 metres from the top of a hill in northern Rangoon. It is built of brick and shaped like an immense cone. Such cone- or bell-shaped pagodas are also called *stupas*. A layer of pure beaten gold covers the shrine from top to bottom. At its base stand much smaller, more delicate stupas.

The main stupa covers a chamber which is believed to hold eight of the Buddha's hairs. For Buddhists, these relics make the shrine especially holy.

At Buddhist festivals, people from all over Burma make pilgrimages to the Shwe Dagon Pagoda. They meditate and worship on the great terrace surrounding the foot of the Golden Pagoda.

◄ WHERE ARE ELEPHANTS USED AS WORKING ANIMALS?

In Asian countries such as India and Burma, elephants are used as beasts of burden.

Trained elephants work mostly at shifting trees that have been felled in forests. They can use their trunks and tusks to lift small logs. Full-grown elephants are strong enough to pull logs weighing up to two tonnes. Young elephants are used mostly for uprooting and clearing away undergrowth.

Each elephant obeys orders given by its trainer, or *mahout*, who sits on its back. Well-trained elephants will kneel, stand and walk, and obey other simple commands.

Unlike horses, and other domesticated animals, elephants do not breed readily in captivity. For this reason, each elephant is captured in the wild and then trained for work. Wild elephants are now in danger of dying out in Asia, so the days of the working elephant might be numbered too.

▶ WHICH CITY HAS 'KLONGS'?

Klongs **are the canals of Bangkok, the capital city of Thailand in South-East Asia.**

Klongs were once so important to life in Bangkok that Western visitors called it 'the Venice of the East'. Throughout the 19th century, most people lived in houses built on stilts driven down into the mud at the edges of canals and the Chao Phraya, the river flowing through Bangkok.

Bangkok had no important roads until 1864, when workers built the Royal Road to connect the king's palace to the buildings downstream where foreign officials lived. By 1910 most people had left the waterside and settled in homes near newly-built roads.

Many Thais still live by the klongs and travel on them. Much of the food and timber from Thailand's farms and forests still reaches Bangkok by canal. A network of canals connects the city to three rivers of the central plain.

◀ WHICH ASIAN CITY AND COUNTRY SHARE THE SAME NAME?

Singapore city is the capital of a tiny South-East Asian country, also called Singapore. The name means 'city of the lions'. Singapore is one of the richest countries in Asia.

The republic of Singapore is a group of small islands just south of the Malay Peninsula. Singapore Island, the largest island, is about the same size as Chicago.

Singapore city stands in the south of Singapore island. It was a small fishing village backed by jungle when British colonists arrived in the 1820s. They made the fine natural harbour into a great port at a cross-roads of trade between East and West.

Today, Singapore city is one of Asia's chief trading and banking centres. There are modern factories, high-rise flats, and skyscraper office blocks. Most of Singapore's population lives and works in the capital.

▶ WHAT ARE CHINESE PAGODAS?

Chinese pagodas are towers with a number of floors, each with its own roof. Pagodas serve as Buddhist shrines.

Pagodas often have eight sides and up to 12 floors. They may be made of wood, brick or stone. Each storey has a roof of coloured, glazed tiles. This curves up at the eaves.

Pagodas are a mixture of Chinese and Indian building styles. The shape of pagodas came from old Chinese watch-towers, which were also built up in stages. But the idea of towers as shrines came from Indian towers and domes called *stupas*. Like stupas, many Chinese pagodas are crowned by what looks like several umbrellas, one above the other. This was a sign that a building had been raised in honour of a royal person.

As long ago as AD 516, the Chinese built a wooden pagoda about 100 metres tall. Most early wooden towers fell down long ago. Some survive in Japan, where this building style was copied.

The tea ceremony is a traditional custom in Japan. The Japanese call it *cha-no-yu*, which means simply 'hot water tea'.

The Japanese tea ceremony is a formal occasion and is carried out according to precise rules. The ceremony is linked to the Zen Buddhist belief that we should find beauty in the ordinary things of daily life.

Tea ceremonies take place in simple, quiet surroundings, often in a special room set aside for the purpose. When the guests have assembled, the hostess begins to prepare the tea with plain, simple utensils. The tea is made by stirring crushed leaves into hot water, and is served in a bowl. After each guest has drunk from the bowl, it is rinsed and filled for the next person.

The atmosphere during the ceremony is serene and peaceful. The guests sit opposite their hostess and talk only of what is taking place during the ritual.

▼ WHICH IS THE WORLD'S BIGGEST CITY?

Tokyo, Peking and Mexico City are all huge. In the early 1980s the city with the most people was Tokyo, the capital of Japan.

Tokyo lies on Tokyo Bay on the east coast of Honshu, the largest Japanese island. It was founded in the 1400s, when it was called Edo.

In 1980, Greater Tokyo had more than 11,350,000 people. But Tokyo and nearby cities had grown so large that they merged. Tokyo and Yokohama, together with their suburbs, form the huge Keihin Metropolitan Area. By the early 1980s, its population was about 28 million. Belgium, in contrast, has ten times the area but a population of only about ten million. Yet Belgium is considered to be a densely-populated country.

Tokyo's industries produce metals, chemicals, machinery, textiles and electronic equipment. The city has more than 200 colleges and universities. Yokohama serves as its port.

▲ WHERE IS GINZA?

Ginza Street, in the Ginza district of Tokyo, is the Japanese capital's great shopping centre. *Ginza* is a Japanese word for silver articles, which craftsmen made there.

Ginza Street runs from north-east to south-west through a part of Tokyo between the Imperial Palace and Tokyo Bay. Nihonbashi Street, at the northern end of Ginza Street, has Tokyo's finest department stores. At night the whole street is brightly lit up.

The Ginza lies close to other important parts of Tokyo. The Emperor lives in the Imperial Palace, nearby. The nearby Marunouchi district is Japan's centre of big business. Government offices and an amusement centre are also not far away.

Much of this area is in the old heart of Tokyo. Fires often burnt down the city's old wooden buildings. After fire destroyed the Ginza in 1872, it was rebuilt in brick from plans drawn up by a British engineer.

▼ WHERE IS THE FORBIDDEN CITY?

The Forbidden City is an old royal part of the Chinese capital Beijing (Peking). Ordinary people were once forbidden to enter buildings in this part of the city.

The Forbidden City (shown here) stands in the centre of the northern half of Beijing. The Forbidden City forms a large square surrounded by a moat 3.2 kilometres long, and a high brick wall.

A gate in the wall leads inside to a number of buildings once used by the Chinese emperors. Imposing throne-halls, roofed with gold tiles, stand on white marble terraces. There are several other palace buildings and courts. These palaces now serve as museums for Chinese works of art. Ordinary Chinese people may now visit this part of Beijing.

Another 'forbidden city' is Lhasa in Tibet. Lhasa was a religious centre for Tibetan Buddhists, and the Tibetans once refused to let Europeans enter the city.

▲ WHICH COUNTRY HAS THE LARGEST POPULATION?

The country with the largest population is the People's Republic of China. By the mid 1980s China had more than 1000 million inhabitants.

China is the world's third largest country after the USSR and Canada, but it has the largest population. One person out of every four on Earth lives in China.

Most Chinese people live in cities and on farms in the valleys and plains of eastern China. Few live in the deserts of the north or the vast mountainous areas of the west.

The Chinese population has grown fast with improved methods of farming and health care. The Chinese are worried by the rate of increase. They fear that there will not be enough food for future generations. The government is trying to reduce the population by discouraging parents from having more than one child.

▼ WHERE DO PEOPLE MAKE GARDENS FROM STONES?

In Japan, gardens are a form of art. Stones, sand and pools of water are carefully arranged to create a landscape of peace and quiet beauty.

The design of Japanese gardens has been influenced by Zen Buddhism. In this school of religion, beauty is seen in simplicity. Long ago, Japanese Zen priests gave special names to rocks set in certain positions. For instance, a garden might include a flat 'worshipping' stone and a tall, solitary 'guardian' stone.

There are two main types of Japanese garden. One is the *hira-niwa* ('level ground'), which has specially arranged rocks set in a bed of raked white sand. The other is the *tsuki-yama* ('artificial hills'), which has hills and ponds. Rocks are chosen to look like distant peaks and mountain slopes. Japanese gardens also have evergreen shrubs and trees, but few flowering plants. The Japanese also make tiny stone gardens in trays. These are called *bon-seki*.

▲ WHERE CAN YOU SEE A KASBAH?

Kasbahs are fortresses. They were built by tribal chieftains in North African countries such as Morocco and Algeria.

Kasbahs are imposing citadels with tall square towers and high walls. Within the walls are living-quarters, storerooms and courtyards.

Many kasbahs were built in the Atlas Mountains by Berbers, the original inhabitants of North Africa. Berber chieftains ruled from kasbahs much as the European barons ruled from their castles in medieval times.

Fortified walled villages are also found close to kasbahs at oases on the edge of the Sahara. They were built of mud, and provided protection against enemy tribes and invaders from the desert.

Famous kasbahs include the residence of the dey, or governor, of Algiers, and the kasbah at Telouet in the High Atlas. A great kasbah at Tifoultout in southern Morocco has been preserved and turned into a hotel.

▲ WHERE ARE SOUKS FOUND?

Souks are Arab markets. North African towns have permanent souks, but in country areas there are weekly market-days.

In North African cities, shops and stalls are set in old, narrow streets, with closely-packed houses. Many houses have a ground-floor workshop, and a shop that opens on to the street. Such shops sell goods that you can see being made in the workshops behind. You can buy anything in a souk, from handmade brassware or carpets to honeyed pastries and spiced roasted meats. Merchants may offer their customers a cup of coffee or a glass of tea while they bargain over an article's price.

Some of Morocco's farming centres are named after their weekly market-day. Thus Souk-el-Khemis means 'Thursday Market'. Weekly markets often take place at deserted spots in the country. Merchants, cobblers, blacksmiths, barbers and villagers flock in on foot, or by bus, to buy and sell.

▼ WHERE IS TIMBUKTU?

Timbuktu is an ancient African town just south of the Sahara Desert. It was once one of the biggest, richest and most famous cities in Africa.

Timbuktu is near the River Niger, in the centre of the republic of Mali. Here the desert meets more fertile land to the south. Timbuktu grew up where farmers met nomads to trade. Its name means 'place of Buktu'. According to legend, a slave called Buktu was left there to mind her nomad owners' possessions.

In the Middle Ages, Timbuktu became famous for gold, salt and slaves. Camel caravans stopped there on long trading treks across the Sahara. By the 1500s, Timbuktu was also a great centre of Muslim learning and had a million inhabitants.

Hundreds of years of warfare followed. Timbuktu was a ruined town when the French conquered it in 1893. Today Timbuktu is a small town of flat-roofed homes built of sun-dried mud brick. It trades mainly in salt.

▶ WHERE IS THE LARGEST AFRICAN NATIONAL PARK?

The largest African national park is the Tsavo National Park in the East African country of Kenya. The park is one of the world's richest wildlife reserves.

Tsavo National Park lies in southern Kenya. The park is slightly larger than the country of Israel. It consists of dry open plains covered with tropical grasses and scrub. Strips of woodland grow along river-banks. There are also long, rocky ridges and lonely outcrops of rock.

Visitors come from all over the world to see the park's many wild mammals and birds. Lions, leopards and cheetahs hunt antelope such as gerenuk, eland and waterbuck. Giraffes, black rhinos and herds of elephants range through the scrub.

There are hundreds of species of birds. They include great eagles, tiny sunbirds, stately herons, colourful weavers and starlings. There are also eight kinds of hornbill. These are birds with huge beaks.

▲ WHERE DO PEOPLE GO ON SAFARI?

'Safari' comes from an Arabic word that means 'of a trip'. Safaris are trips made to hunt or watch wild animals, especially in East Africa.

Until recently, hunters used to go on safari to kill the big game that teemed in what are now Kenya, Uganda and Tanzania. White and black hunters and farmers killed so many animals that some species became rare. Many animals now live in protected national parks or game reserves.

The most famous parks include Kenya's Tsavo National Park and Tanzania's Serengeti National Park and Ngorongoro Crater. Here people go on safari with cameras, not guns. They watch and film the wildlife instead of shooting to kill. Many visitors arrive by bus or plane.

Although some rare kinds of animals are now protected by law, many are still killed by poachers. African elephants, for example, are slaughtered for their valuable ivory tusks.

▲ WHERE ARE THE OLDEST CHURCHES IN AFRICA?

Africa's oldest surviving churches stand in north-east Africa, in the ancient African country of Ethiopia.

Christianity reached what is now Ethiopia in the fourth century AD, but the best-known Ethiopian churches are about eight centuries old. Eleven of them stand at the small town of Lalibela in the mountains of north-central Ethiopia. Workers carved the churches out of solid rock.

The largest church is the Medhane Alem ('The Saviour of the World'). It measures 33 metres in length and 11 metres in height. Its roof is level with the top of the rest of the rock from which it was carved. A deep trench separates the church from the natural rock.

Ethiopian builders might have learned this way of building from Indian architects. Legend has it that King Lalibela had most of these churches built between 1181 and 1221.

**Oases are moist places in
deserts. Here, plants grow
and there may be enough
food and water for passers-
by or people making a
permanent home.**

Oases are found in the Sahara,
Gobi and other great deserts of
the world. They occur
wherever the ground holds a
good supply of fresh water.

In North American deserts,
oases are often found in valleys
where water soaks into the soil
after running off mountains.
In the Sahara Desert there are
oases where springs bubble up,
or where underground streams
or layers of water lie high
enough to be reached by
digging a well.

Oases vary in size and shape.
Some are just a clump of trees
around a small spring. The
Nile Valley in Egypt is a
narrow oasis hundreds of
kilometres long. The River
Nile waters crops which are
planted along its banks. This
huge oasis grows enough food
for millions of people. Tropical
oases produce crops such as
dates, rice and wheat.

**The longest canal able to
take large sea-going ships is
the Suez Canal. This passes
through Egypt to connect the
Mediterranean Sea and the
Red Sea.**

The Suez Canal measures 160
kilometres. It joins the cities of
Port Said in the north and Suez
in the south. Between the cities
it crosses the Isthmus of Suez,
a narrow neck of land that
links Africa to Asia. The canal
passes through several lakes,

**Benin was an old kingdom in
West Africa. Its centre lay in
what is now south-west
Nigeria, not the modern
country of Benin.**

including the Bitter Lakes, on
the way.

The French engineer
Ferdinand de Lesseps had the
canal built between 1859 and
1869. It shortened the voyage
from Britain to India by 5600
kilometres.

At first, the waterway was
only 8 metres deep and 22
metres wide at the bottom. As
larger ships began to be built,
the canal became too shallow
and narrow. It is now being
widened and deepened so that
it can take ships designed for
loads of 225,000 tonnes.

The Negro kingdom of Benin
gave its name to the forested
coastland of what are now
eastern Ghana, Togo, Benin
and Nigeria. Benin reached its
peak of power and prosperity
between the 1300s and 1600s.

By the late 1400s the *oba*, or
king, of Benin controlled an
empire stretching for hundreds
of kilometres with the help of
his well-trained army. The
capital was Benin City. About
80,000 people lived there in
neat rows of huts surrounded
by a wall and a moat. Many
were skilled craftsmen. Benin
metal workers cast fine heads
in bronze and brass, like the
one shown here.

Benin City became an
important centre of trade
between inland Negroes and
Europeans on the coast. But by
the late 1800s wars and slave-
raiding had made Benin poor
and weak.

▼ WHERE IS GREAT ZIMBABWE?

Great Zimbabwe is a ruined stone city in southern Africa. Its name means 'Houses of Stone'.

Great Zimbabwe stands in a valley among rocky hills in south-east Zimbabwe. The roofless ruins consist of granite blocks piled up without the use of cement. There are three groups of buildings, known as the Acropolis, Valley Ruins and Temple. The Acropolis has massive walls and a maze of corridors and curved stairs. The Valley Ruins are smaller buildings. The Temple's high walls enclose a mysterious solid tower.

Archaeologists think that Bantu-speaking Shona Negroes built Great Zimbabwe between AD 1200 and 1450. The Shonas' rulers grew rich by trading in gold. These priest-kings probably lived in Great Zimbabwe. Its high walls hid them from the gaze of the people, for Shonas worshipped their priest-kings almost as if they were gods.

▶ WHERE ARE THE VICTORIA FALLS?

The Victoria Falls are a great waterfall in south-central Africa. They stand on the Zambezi River where it flows between Zambia and Zimbabwe.

The Zambezi is about 1.6 kilometres wide at the falls. Here the river plunges over a cliff of hard volcanic rock up to 108 metres in depth. Below the falls the river flows on through a deep, narrow gorge worn by the falling water. This gorge is 64 kilometres long. In all Africa, only the Boyoma Falls on the Zaire River carry more water.

As the water crashes down, it hurls a cloud of spray and mist high in the air. People can see it from miles away. Local Africans called the falls *Mosi-*

oa-tunya ('The Smoke that Thunders'). The Scottish explorer David Livingstone was the first European to see the falls, in 1855. He named them after Queen Victoria of Britain.

▼ WHERE DO ZULUS LIVE?

Zulus are a Bantu-speaking Negro people who live in part of eastern South Africa. They were once famous as warriors.

More than five million Zulus live in the north-east of the South African province of Natal. Their homeland is usually called Zululand, but the South African government uses the name KwaZulu ('the Zulu nation') for the Zulus' own territory.

Zulus are strongly built people. They live in *kraals*, villages with cattle pens surrounded by huts. Young men once formed regiments called *impis*. These worked and fought for the Zulu king.

In the early 1800s the Zulus were a small, local tribe. Then their chief, Shaka, built up a powerful army of warriors armed with light stabbing spears called *assegais*. His troops terrified neighbouring tribes and mastered all of what is now Natal. In 1879 the Zulus, led by their king, Cetewayo, fought British troops in the Zulu War. The Zulus were defeated.

◄ WHERE IS THE STATUE OF LIBERTY?

This immense statue rises from Liberty Island in New York Harbor. It is one of the world's tallest statues.

The statue shows a woman wearing a robe and holding a huge burning torch aloft in her right hand. The left hand holds a tablet bearing the date of the American Declaration of Independence (1776).

The figure is made of thin copper sheets fixed over an iron framework held up by steel columns. It weighs over 200 tonnes and rises 46 metres from an immense pedestal which is 47 metres high.

People can climb up inside the statue by means of a lift and a spiral stairway. At night the torch shines with a powerful light and the statue is floodlit.

The French sculptor Frédéric-Auguste Bartholdi designed the statue. It was made in France as a gift from France to the United States. The statue arrived there by ship in separate pieces in 1885.

◄ WHERE IS MANHATTAN?

Manhattan is an island in New York State. It forms the heart of New York city.

Manhattan Island is a narrow island about 21 kilometres long and 3.2 kilometres wide. It lies east of the Hudson River, and west of the East River, with New York Bay to the south and the Harlem River to the north.

The island is one of the world's great business and cultural centres. Some of the world's tallest skyscraper buildings tower over the south of Manhattan. Manhattan also has the famous theatres of Broadway, New York's Stock Exchange and the smart stores of Fifth Avenue. Its best-known landmarks include the United Nations Building, the American Museum of Natural History, the Metropolitan Museum of Art and Central Park.

Indians called the island *Man-a-hat-ta*, meaning 'Heavenly Land'. Dutch colonists bought it from them in 1626 for a handful of cloth and trinkets.

◄ WHERE IS THE WHITE HOUSE?

The White House stands in Washington, DC, the capital of the United States. It is the official residence of the president of the USA.

The White House stands on Pennsylvania Avenue amid lawns, trees and flowerbeds. Each year more than a million people visit parts of the house open to the public.

The imposing main building has a great porch like the front of an ancient temple. Inside are richly decorated state rooms. The president lives in rooms above.

Long, low galleries jut out to the east and west. Beyond lie the West and East wings. The West Wing contains offices where the president and his staff work. Other staff work in the East Wing.

Construction of the White House began in 1792. It was rebuilt and enlarged after the British burnt it in 1814. The name first came from its white limestone walls, which were later painted white to hide the fire damage.

▶ WHERE IS CAPE CANAVERAL?

Cape Canaveral is a low sandy cape in the south-east United States. It is the main launch site for American spacecraft and long-range missiles.

Cape Canaveral stands on the east coast of Florida. Its John F. Kennedy Space Center includes the Launch Operations Center of the National Aeronautics and Space Administration (NASA), and the first tracking station of the Atlantic Missile Range.

The first American satellite was launched from Cape Canaveral. In 1969 Neil Armstrong and Edwin Aldrin left the cape to become the first people on the Moon. Also at the cape is the start of a missile-testing range that extends across the South Atlantic Ocean.

Visitors to the cape can see space rockets on show, and the building used for assembling the Apollo spacecraft. The Space Shuttle is also launched from Cape Canaveral.

▶ WHERE IS DISNEYLAND?

Disneyland is the world's best-known amusement park. The American film producer Walt Disney built it at Anaheim in California. Disneyland is about 40 kilometres south-east of Los Angeles.

Some people rate Disneyland as one of the seven wonders of the modern world. Millions of parents and children go there each year from all over the world to enjoy the park's main amusement areas. These are Adventureland, Frontierland, Fantasyland and Tomorrowland.

Visitors enjoy a huge range of attractions. They can bobsleigh down a miniature Matterhorn mountain, speed through outer space, glide under the ocean by submarine, visit a haunted house, explore the old frontier, go on a jungle safari, or be fired on by pirates.

Among the most popular sights are daily parades that include Disney cartoon characters. Many events have been added since Disneyland opened in 1955.

▶ WHERE IS THE LONGEST ARTIFICIAL SEAWAY?

The longest artificial seaway is the St Lawrence Seaway. This allows ocean-going ships to sail from the Atlantic Ocean to the Great Lakes deep in North America.

The St Lawrence Seaway runs for about 300 kilometres along the St Lawrence River, which flows from Lake Ontario to the Atlantic Ocean. To make the seaway, engineers dredged stretches of river to deepen them. They cut new canals and deepened the old Welland Canal. They also built locks as giant 'lifts' to raise and lower ships from one water level to another.

American and Canadian teams made the seaway, which largely lies between Ontario in Canada and New York State in the United States. It opened in 1959. Big ships using it can sail more than 3700 kilometres inland from the Atlantic to a port on Lake Superior. The photograph shows the seaway as it passes through the city of Quebec.

▼ WHERE DID THE OLMECS LIVE?

The Olmecs were Stone-Age Indians who lived in Mexico. Their civilization was among the first in Central America.

The Olmec culture flourished about 1100–800 BC in central Mexico and south far into Guatemala. *Olmec* means 'rubber people', a name first used for Indians in south-east Mexico, where rubber trees were plentiful.

The Olmecs lacked metal tools, yet carved hard stone with skill. They made stone jaguars, dwarfs and huge human heads. The largest head weighs 15 tonnes and stands about 2.7 metres high. Its thick lips and flat nose are unlike those of modern Indians.

The Olmecs made delicate objects too, such as finely ground and polished stone mirrors. Their carvings suggest that they worshipped a god shown as half jaguar, half human.

The Olmecs had a type of early writing and probably knew a way of measuring the year.

▼ WHERE ARE FOUR AMERICAN PRESIDENTS CARVED OUT OF ROCK?

These immense carvings are cut in the Black Hills of South Dakota, in the midwest United States. They rank among the world's largest sculptures.

The carvings jut from a granite cliff called Mount Rushmore, which is 40 kilometres south-east of Rapid City. Seen from below, the carvings show the heads of four past presidents of the USA: George Washington, Thomas Jefferson, Theodore Roosevelt and Abraham Lincoln. The four giant heads are about 18 metres high and can be seen from a distance of 97 kilómetres. The whole group is known as the Mount Rushmore National Memorial.

The American sculptor Gutzon Borglum planned the memorial. Work started in 1927 and lasted into the 1960s. Workmen used drills and dynamite to cut into the cliff face. They had small model faces to guide them as they worked.

▲ WHICH CITY HAS FLOATING GARDENS?

Mexico City, the capital of Mexico, has floating gardens. You can see them at Xochimilco, a southern suburb of Mexico City.

Xochimilco stands on the shores of Lake Xochimilco, and the floating gardens lie on this lake. Xochimilco is an Indian word that means 'place of flowers'.

Long ago, local Indians grew flowers and vegetables on rafts moored out on the lake. They made these rafts of reeds and twigs woven together and covered with mud. In time, plant roots grew down from the rafts into the bed of the lake.

Today, these floating gardens look like meadows rimmed with flowers and poplar trees. The strips of lake water between the 'meadows' resemble canals.

Thousands of tourists visit the gardens each year. Many travel the waterways in canoes decorated with flowers. They punt the canoes along with oars.

▼ WHERE DO NORTH AMERICAN INDIANS LIVE?

In the United States and Canada many Indians live on land set aside for them by the government. These lands are called reserves in Canada and reservations in the United States.

The United States has over 100 reservations and there are more than 2000 reserves in Canada. Indians do not have to live on these lands, but may avoid paying tax if they do.

Many Indians hunt or farm,

or raise livestock on their tribe's land. Others leave their homes and work in mines, factories or farms elsewhere. Indians living on reserves are often poorer than most North Americans but some tribal lands are rich in minerals or timber.

Reservations and reserves vary greatly in size. The largest reservation is that of the Navaho tribe in Arizona and New Mexico. It is bigger than Portugal in area. The Navaho women in the photograph are weaving rugs on a hand-loom.

▼ WHERE ARE TOTEM POLES FOUND?

Totem poles are tall, straight tree trunks carved usually to look like human and animal figures perched one on top of another. They were made by Indians in North America.

Each totem pole showed a totem. A totem is an animal representing a clan, or group of families. In some societies people worship their totem and have rules to forbid killing that kind of animal. Some people also believe that the totem animal is their ancestor.

The tallest totem pole was raised at Alert Bay in Vancouver Island, Canada, in 1973. It is 52.7 metres high. The area is the home of the Kwakiutl Indians, who were making totem poles hundreds of years ago. This pole's carvings tell the story of the Kwakiutl.

The Kwakiutl used to raise totem poles at a feast called a potlatch, which lasted for several days. To show off his importance, the host of the potlatch would give away vast quantities of his possessions to the guests.

▼ WHERE IS MESA VERDE?

Mesa Verde is a national park in south-western Colorado, in the United States. It is famous for Indian cliff-dwellings.

Mesa Verde means 'green table'. This name comes from the park's forested hills with flat tops and steep sides like the walls of deep canyons.

Centuries ago, Indians built villages against the undercut walls. The overhanging rock above helped to protect these so-called Cliff-Dwellers from

enemy tribes.

Cliff Palace, Long House and Spruce Tree House are names of some of the Cliff-Dwellers' villages. Cliff Palace was the largest. This held up to 400 Indians who lived in 200 rooms built of stone and sun-dried mud. In places, as many as four rooms are built on top of each other. There are also special pit houses called *kivas* where Cliff-Dwellers held religious ceremonies.

Indians probably built most of the cliff-dwellings in the twelfth century AD. Drought drove them out by AD 1300.

▼ WHERE IS THE LAND OF FIRE?

'Land of Fire' is the English translation of *Tierra del Fuego*. This is the name of a group of islands at the southern tip of South America.

Tierra del Fuego is a little smaller than Ireland. Most of it is one island, also called Tierra del Fuego. Beyond the Strait of Magellan lies mainland South America.

The name of the islands is misleading. They are often wretchedly wet, windy and cold. Indeed the name 'Land of Fire' comes from bonfires once kept alight by Indians trying to stay warm. The Portuguese explorer Ferdinand Magellan glimpsed these fires in 1520 when he became the first European to sail through the Strait of Magellan.

Today the strait and the western part of the island group belong to Chile. Argentina owns the eastern part of the main island. Ushaia, on the Chilean part of this island, is the world's southernmost city.

▶ WHERE DO GAUCHOS LIVE?

Gauchos are South American cowboys. They work on cattle ranches on the pampas, the grassy plains of Argentina and Uruguay.

Gauchos were once wandering cowboys who were their own masters. They wore a broad-brimmed hat, colourful scarf, bright shirt, wide silver belt, baggy trousers and high leather boots.

These men were skilled horsemen famed for toughness and bravery. They became expert at catching cows by throwing the *bola*. This was a kind of sling that wrapped itself around the legs of a running cow, tripping it up.

Early gauchos were half Indian, half Spanish. They lived by catching and selling wild cattle. Later, most worked for men who had built up big cattle herds. When farmers fenced in the open range, gauchos lost their old free-roaming way of life. Many became farmhands or soldiers. Today, few of the old-style gauchos are left.

▲ WHICH IS THE HIGHEST CAPITAL CITY?

La Paz, in the South American country of Bolivia, is higher than any other city used as a centre of government.

La Paz is about 3660 metres above sea level. It stands near Lake Titicaca, in the Andes Mountains of western Bolivia. Snow-capped peaks tower high above the city.

More than half a million people live in La Paz. Many work for the government or in factories making products such as flour, beer or leather.

Spanish colonists founded La Paz in 1548. (*Paz* means 'Peace'.) The town of Sucre is Bolivia's official capital, but La Paz is the centre of government. Its population is just over half a million.

► WHERE HAS BRASÍLIA BEEN BUILT?

Brasília is a city built in east-central Brazil. In 1960 it replaced Rio de Janeiro as Brazil's centre of government.

Brasília stands on a plateau about 965 kilometres north-west of Rio de Janeiro. By building a new capital in the interior, Brasília's planners hoped to open up the undeveloped heart of the country.

Many cities grow gradually, according to no particular plan, but Brasília was carefully designed and built. Lucio Costa planned its layout to look like a huge cross. The Brazilian architect Oscar Niemeyer designed the main buildings. Many are tall slabs of concrete and glass. Buildings housing the three areas of government meet at the Plaza of Three Powers, which is a huge triangular space.

Construction of Brasília began in the late 1950s. Its population is now approaching one million.

▲ WHERE IS THE MOST COLOURFUL CARNIVAL HELD?

New Orleans and Nice are among cities with famous carnivals; but perhaps the most colourful carnival takes place in Rio de Janeiro, on the south-east coast of Brazil.

Rio de Janeiro's citizens hold their carnival each year just before Lent. Almost everyone gets involved. Clubs and societies prepare months ahead. They hold contests to find the best new songs and the best fancy dress costumes.

At carnival time, gaily coloured flags and lights hang from the buildings. Thousands of singing, dancing citizens take to the streets, together with bands and displays borne through the streets on wheeled platforms. For a while, rich and poor alike celebrate the carnival.

Even outside carnival time there is much to enjoy in this great city. Gleaming white beaches and tall mountain peaks make Rio de Janeiro one of the world's most spectacular cities. Soaring above the city are the high peaks of Sugar Loaf Mountain (395 metres) and Corcovado (704 metres). At the summit of Corcovado is the statue of Christ the Redeemer, which is 30 metres high. Famous beaches in Rio de Janeiro include those of Ipanema and Copacabana.

Rio de Janeiro is also a great port and business centre. But there are shacks as well as fine buildings. Thousands of extremely poor people live in slums on hills at the fringe of the city centre.

▼ WHICH COUNTRY IS THE WORLD'S LARGEST WOOL PRODUCER?

Australia produces more wool than any other country. More than a quarter of the world's wool comes from Australian sheep.

Australia produces so much wool because much of the country is suited for sheep raising. There are rich pastures and vast areas of grassland too dry for crops. Between them, both types of grassland can support 150 million or more sheep. This is more than ten sheep for every Australian person.

Australia's best-known wool producer is the Merino. This is a hardy, heavy-fleeced breed of sheep suited to hot, dry climates. Thanks to the Merino, Australia can produce more than 700,000 tonnes of wool in one year.

Other breeds are kept more for their meat. Australia is one of the world's top producers of mutton and lamb.

Drought sometimes destroys huge areas of grass. Then thousands of sheep may die of hunger and thirst.

▼ WHERE IS THE NULLARBOR PLAIN?

This great treeless plain got its name from the Latin words *nulla arbor*, meaning 'no tree'. The Nullarbor Plain lies in southern Australia close to the Great Australian Bight.

The Nullarbor Plain covers parts of the states of Western and South Australia. The plain is larger than Yugoslavia, and nearly as big as New Zealand.

The plain is low, flat and monotonous. Little rain falls.

▲ WHICH IS THE LARGEST AUSTRALIAN CITY?

The largest Australian city is Sydney, capital of the state of New South Wales. It has a population of over three million.

When it does rain, the water sinks down through holes in the rock, which is limestone, and forms underground lakes. There are no surface rivers, and the only plants to thrive are hardy shrubs such as saltbush.

There are only a few settlements along the Eyre highway and the trans-Australia railway, which both cross the Nullarbor Plain. The world's longest straight stretch of rail is 478 kilometres of track across the plain. The Nullarbor Plain is also the site of a rocket research centre.

Sydney stands on the south-east coast of Australia, on one of the world's finest natural harbours. This is a series of deep-water inlets opening on the Pacific Ocean.

Sydney began in 1788 as a British prison settlement. It has grown into one of Australia's chief centres for business, manufacturing and the arts. The city makes ships, cars, textiles, chemical products and processed food. Its port exports farm products.

The city's famous buildings include Sydney Harbour Bridge, one of the world's largest steel-arch bridges. This links the main city centre with suburbs on the northern shore of the harbour. Sydney Opera House, which was completed in 1973, overlooks the harbour. The white arches of its roof resemble the billowing sails of yachts.

▼ WHERE IS AYERS ROCK?

Ayers Rock is an immense stone outcrop near the centre of Australia. It is famous as the largest rock on the Earth's surface.

Ayers Rock stands in the Northern Territory, about 440 kilometres south-west of the town of Alice Springs. The rock is about 2.4 kilometres long, 1.6 kilometres wide, and 8 kilometres around the base. It rises to a height of 335 metres from a low, sandy plain where only small, tough plants grow. The rock was left exposed after surrounding layers of rock were worn away by erosion.

From the air, the rock looks like a great stranded whale. At sunset, its bare sandstone slopes glow brilliant orange. Then they turn purple as the light starts to fade.

Long ago, Australian Aborigines made paintings on the walls of the caves in the rock. The first Europeans to see Ayers Rock arrived in 1872. Today, thousands of visitors to central Australia visit this huge outcrop.

▲ WHERE DID THE PEOPLE OF THE PACIFIC ISLANDS COME FROM?

Long ago, Stone-Age peoples settled in thousands of islands far out in the Pacific Ocean. Groups reached the islands by canoe at different times from Asia.

There are three great groups of Pacific Islands, mostly in the South Pacific. The south-west group is Melanesia, or the 'black islands'. Their black-skinned islanders have frizzy hair and look like Negroes. Their ancestors may have come from Indonesia.

The north-west Pacific Islands are called Micronesia, or 'little islands'. The Micronesians are tall with light-brown skin. Micronesians probably spread east from South-East Asia.

Most islands east of Melanesia and Micronesia belong to Polynesia, or 'the many islands'. Polynesians are tall and strongly built, with paler skins than the other islanders. Finds of old tools show that the early Polynesians most likely came from southern China.

▲ WHERE IS THE AUSTRALIAN 'OUTBACK'?

The 'outback' is a name for the remote, wild interior of Australia. Few people live in the outback. Most Australians live in towns and cities near the coast.

The Australian outback has a dry climate, and deserts cover much of the country. These bare lands include immense level plains where little but eucalyptus and acacia scrub grows. After the rains, desert areas are often covered with carpets of wild flowers.

In areas with more rainfall, there are vast sheep and cattle stations. In some rainier parts of the outback, near the coast, there are forests of giant eucalyptus trees.

Early explorers and settlers saw the outback as a place of adventure. But some died of hunger or thirst, lost in its deserts, or killed by its droughts. Even now, only skilled Aborigine hunters and food-gatherers can survive without help in Australia's harsh, dry heartland.

▶ WHERE IS THE LONGEST BRIDGE?

The answer depends on how you measure bridge length. In the early 1980s the bridge with the greatest length between supports was the Humber Estuary Bridge in the north-east of England.

The Humber Estuary Bridge crosses the River Humber's estuary near Hull in Humberside. This suspension bridge has a main span that measures 1410 metres in length. The span is slung from cables supported by two giant towers. Each tower rises to a height of more than 162 metres. Because the Earth's surface is curved, the towers are slightly farther apart at the top than at the bottom.

Including its two side spans, the Humber Estuary Bridge measures 2220 metres in length. This is 323 metres shorter than the Mackinac Straits Bridge in Michigan.

Work on the Humber Bridge lasted from 1972 to 1980. Engineers first built foundations for the towers and anchorages at the ends of the bridge. Then they put up the towers. Next they hung the main cables and anchored them at each end of the bridge. Lastly they slung the roadway in place.

▶ WHICH IS THE LARGEST COUNTRY?

The world's largest country is the USSR (Union of Soviet Socialist Republics), or Soviet Union for short. The USSR is more than twice the size of Canada, the second largest country.

REPUBLICS OF THE USSR

Russian SFSR (1)	Turkmenistan (5)	Tadzhikistan (9)	Lithuania (13)
Kazakhstan (2)	Armenia (6)	Ukraine (10)	Byelorussia (14)
Uzbekistan (3)	Georgia (7)	Estonia (11)	Moldavia (15)
Kirgizia (4)	Azerbaijan (8)	Latvia (12)	

The USSR covers more than 22,200 million square kilometres. It includes more than half of Europe and almost two-fifths of Asia. This makes the USSR larger than four of the world's seven continents.

The USSR stretches from the Baltic and Black seas in the west to the Pacific Ocean in the east. To the north is the Arctic Ocean and to the south are the countries of Turkey, Iran, Afghanistan, Mongolia and China.

Within the USSR there are many types of climate and countryside. In the north are vast areas of cold, treeless tundra and huge evergreen forests. Farther south are grasslands, mountains and deserts.

There are 15 republics in the USSR with their own cultures and languages. The largest is Russia, which stretches from Europe to Siberia. Russians make up more than half the population of the USSR. The capital city, Moscow, lies in Russia, and the official language of the USSR is Russian.

▲ WHERE IS THE TALLEST BUILDING?

▲ WHERE IS THE LONGEST ROAD TUNNEL?

▲ WHICH IS THE SMALLEST COUNTRY?

The world's tallest office building is the Sears Tower, in Chicago, Illinois. Its highest roof level rises 443 metres above the ground.

The Sears Tower stands on Wacker Drive in Chicago's central business district. Here land is so expensive that people build offices upward rather than outward.

The tower is an office block that looks like nine upended narrow glass boxes, some longer than others, joined at the sides. Steel frames inside support the walls, which are made of aluminium and dark glass. The building has 110 floors, 16,000 windows, 103 lifts, and 18 escalators. More than 16,500 people work in it.

The Sears Tower is named after a mail-order firm called Sears, Roebuck and Company, which had it built between 1970 and 1973. Some television masts and towers are even taller than the Sears Tower.

The world's longest road tunnel is the St Gotthard Road Tunnel which runs beneath the Swiss Alps.

The St Gotthard Road Tunnel is in southern Switzerland. It runs for 16.3 kilometres from Göschenen south to Airolo. The tunnel cuts through a huge mountain mass called the St Gotthard Massif.

This mountain mass had always hindered travellers journeying through Switzerland on their way between Germany and Italy. After 1882 the St Gotthard Rail Tunnel made travel easier, but the only road wound over a mountain pass made dangerous by deep snow in winter.

Cutting the St Gotthard Road Tunnel began in 1970. Engineers worked toward each other from both ends. They met in 1976, and the two-lane tunnel opened in 1980.

The new road tunnel takes two hours off the road journey from north to south Switzerland. The tunnel is open all the year.

The world's smallest country is Vatican City, the Pope's official home. This country is an independent state within the country of Italy.

The Vatican stands in the city of Rome. It covers only 0.44 square kilometres, and is no bigger than many parks. Only about 700 people live in Vatican City.

The Vatican's main buildings are St Peter's (the world's largest church) and the Vatican Palace, which has over a thousand rooms. There are chapels, apartments, offices, and a museum, library, and collection of documents.

Officials run the state's daily affairs. There is a governor, as well as a cardinal secretary of state, experts in law and money management, and legates (ambassadors) who go abroad.

The Vatican has its own police. The Swiss Guards, who wear uniforms of a style unchanged for centuries, act as the Pope's bodyguard. The Vatican issues its own stamps and newspapers.

WHERE WERE THE SEVEN WONDERS OF THE WORLD?

These famous structures were built in lands near the eastern end of the Mediterranean Sea in ancient times. Antipater of Sidon drew up the list in the second century BC.

The Pyramids of Egypt were the tombs of Egyptian pharaohs. The Hanging Gardens of Babylon were terraced gardens in what is now Iraq. The Statue of Zeus at Olympia stood in Greece at the site of the first Olympic Games. It was 12 metres high and made of ivory, gold and gems. The Temple of Diana was a great marble temple built at Ephesus in what is now western Turkey. Also in Turkey was the Mausoleum of Halicarnassus, a tomb made for King Mausolus. The Colossus of Rhodes was a giant statue on the island of Rhodes. The Pharos of Alexandria was an Egyptian lighthouse which may have been 122 metres high. Of all these ancient structures, only the pyramids still exist.

WHERE IS EASTER ISLAND?

Easter Island is a small, remote island in the South Pacific. It is famous for its mysterious giant stone heads and a strange writing system, both made by Stone-Age peoples.

Easter Island lies 3860 kilometres west of Chile and nearly half as far from Pitcairn, the nearest inhabited island.

Polynesians settled on Easter Island more than a thousand years ago. Their descendants built great stone burial platforms around the coast. On these they raised immense carved human heads, each weighing up to 50 tonnes. The Easter Islanders probably achieved this with just stone picks, ropes, ramps and pebble rollers. Easter Islanders also devised the *rongorongo* picture script, which no one can now decipher.

By 1872 wars, slave raids and disease had almost wiped out the islanders. But legends and finds of ancient tools have helped archaeologists to piece together some of the island's past.

Pyramids of Egypt

Statue of Zeus at Olympia

Mausoleum of Halicarnassus

Temple of Diana

Pharos of Alexandria

Colossus of Rhodes

Hanging Gardens of Babylon

▼ WHERE IS THE HOME OF THE YETI?

The yeti is an ape-like beast which is supposed to live high up in the Himalaya Mountains of Asia.

The yeti is also known as the Abominable Snowman. Mountain people say that it lives on high snowy slopes, but will move down to attack villagers. They describe it as big, ape-like and hairy, with arms that hang to its knees. It supposedly walks upright on sturdy legs, like a human.

Tribespeople claim to have seen this creature, but no one has ever proved it exists. The British mountaineer Eric Shipton photographed 'yeti' tracks which he found in snow near Mount Everest in 1951. But such big footprints could have been made by a bear. In 1954, the members of another expedition examined three 'yeti' scalps which in fact had come from a rare goat-like mammal known as the serow.

Some people believe that the yeti may be a type of early human which has survived in the Himalayas to the present-day.

▼ WHERE IS THE BERMUDA TRIANGLE?

The Bermuda Triangle is a popular name for a triangular patch of the Atlantic Ocean off the south-east United States. There are claims that many ships and planes have disappeared or met with unexplained accidents in the area of the triangle.

People disagree about the exact area of the triangle. Some suggest that its corners are formed by Florida and the islands of Bermuda and Puerto Rico.

More than 50 ships and 20 planes are said to have vanished inside the triangle. This is far more than you might expect for an area this size. In one disaster, five American bombers disappeared together in 1945. Tales also tell of crews missing from boats found with hot meals aboard.

Writers blame the disappearances on underwater volcanoes, strange forces or death rays from space. But storms, human error and mechanical faults could have caused the incidents.

▼ WHERE WAS ATLANTIS?

According to legend, Atlantis was a powerful island kingdom that used to lie in the Atlantic Ocean. Then, one day, it sank. Archaeologists think a real island gave rise to this legend.

The Greek philosopher Plato described Atlantis more than 2300 years ago. Long before that, he declared, Atlantis had been a great island empire. Its armies overran many Mediterranean lands but were defeated by Athens. Later, earthquakes and floods struck Atlantis, and it sank swiftly under the sea.

Many people have believed that this story is true. Some thought that Atlantis was really America, the Canary Islands or the Bahamas.

In the 1960s, Greek archaeologists discovered that an ancient civilization had once flourished on a volcanic island known as Thera, or Santorini, in the Aegean Sea. In about 1450 BC the volcano exploded, destroying the civilization. It is possible that Thera was Atlantis.

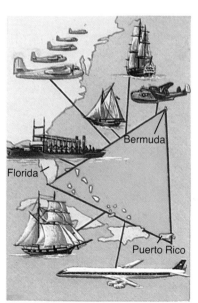

Bermuda

Florida

Puerto Rico

TRANSPORT

▼ WHERE ARE THE WORLD'S BUSIEST SEA LANES?

The busiest sea lanes are narrow seas where many ships carry cargo and passengers to and from industrial nations.

The English Channel between France and England is one of the busiest sea lanes in the world. The English Channel is about 563 kilometres long and no more than 34 kilometres wide at its narrowest, between Dover and Cap Gris-Nez. The Channel joins the Atlantic Ocean to the North Sea.

Each day, dozens of big cargo ships sail through the Channel to and from the great ports of northern Europe. The ships include oil tankers and container vessels. Between them they carry huge loads of food, fuel, minerals and manufactured goods.

▼ WHERE ARE THE MAIN OIL SEA-ROUTES?

Thousands of miles of sea separate many oil-producing countries from the chief oil-consuming countries. The main oil sea-routes cross the oceans between them.

Oil sea-routes run from oil-producing countries such as Saudi Arabia and Iran (on the Persian Gulf), Indonesia, Libya in North Africa, and Venezuela in South America. The routes lead to major oil consumers such as the United States, the nations of Western Europe and Japan.

One of the main oil routes leads from the Persian Gulf down the coast of East Africa, then around Africa's southern tip and up the west coast to North America and Western Europe. Oil routes sailed by supertankers end at deep-water offshore terminals.

▼ WHERE IS THE WORLD'S BUSIEST PORT?

The busiest port is the Rotterdam-Europoort in the Netherlands. This handles more cargo than any other port in the world.

The Rotterdam-Europoort lies on the Nieuwe Maas, a branch of the River Rhine. The New Waterway canal links it with the North Sea, 29 kilometres away. The port covers about 100 square kilometres and is the largest artificial harbour. Waterways link the Rotterdam-Europoort with other parts of the Netherlands and with German cities on the Rhine.

By the early 1980s this port was handling from 253 to 286 million tonnes of seaborne cargo every year. More than 29,000 sea-going ships and up to 200,000 barges were annually using Rotterdam.

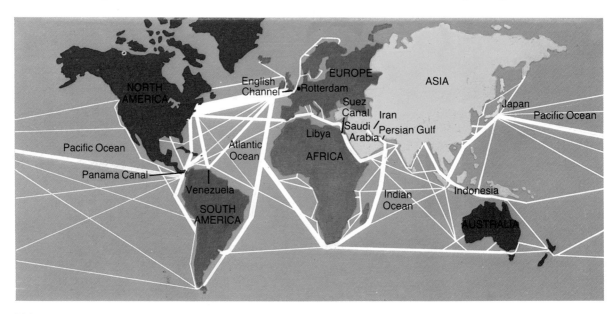

▼ WHERE DO ICEBREAKERS OPERATE?

Icebreakers are ships that operate where waterways freeze over thickly. They break the ice to let other ships through. At least one Russian icebreaker can crush ice four metres thick.

Icebreakers open passages through ice-covered lakes and seas. They work in the Great Lakes, the Baltic Sea and around the Arctic Ocean.

An icebreaker has a strong, heavy bow, armoured sides and powerful engines. The bow is deeply undercut so that it can rear up on to the ice. The ship's crew pump water into forward tanks. This makes the bow heavy enough to crush the ice by sheer weight. The crew can also break the ice by shifting water inside the ship to make it rock from side to side.

Icebreakers have hulls especially strengthened and shaped to resist ice pressing in from the sides. The hulls must be broader than those of following ships, to leave them a wide enough passage.

▲ WHERE ARE LIGHTHOUSES BUILT?

Lighthouses are built mostly on or near coastal reefs and peninsulas, and at harbours and ports. Some lighthouses warn sailors of danger. Others help to guide them to a safe anchorage.

Lighthouses have been used for centuries to guide and warn sailors. The most famous ancient lighthouse was the Pharos of Alexandria, built in Egypt about 300 BC.

Early lighthouses were just wooden towers with metal baskets of burning wood or coal hung from poles on top. Many modern lighthouses are built of cast iron or reinforced concrete. Their lights are magnified by lenses so that they can be seen from great distances. The most powerful of all lights shines from the Creac'h d'Ouessant lighthouse. This warns of treacherous rocks off north-west France.

Most lighthouses have sirens that blare out coded fog-warnings. Some emit radio signals to guide ships with radio direction finders.

At anchor Port side

Starboard side Vessels approaching

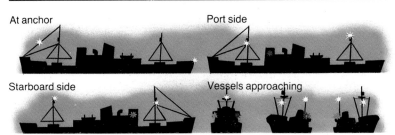

▲ WHERE ARE THE NAVIGATION LIGHTS ON A SHIP?

This depends mostly on what the ship is doing and partly on the size of the ship.

The main navigation lights for a moving ship are the masthead light, sidelights and sternlight. Ships with hulls of 50 metres or more show two white masthead lights. The foremast light is 6.12 metres above the hull and is visible from ahead and either side. The mainmast light is higher than the foremast light and is visible for ten kilometres.

There are two sidelights. The port light (left side) is red and the starboard light (right side) is green. Sidelights are lower than masthead lights and are also visible from ahead. The sternlight (at the back) is white.

Anchored vessels show one or more white lights, and light up their decks if they measure 100 metres or more. Ships that are towing show a yellow light at the stern.

▶ WHERE IS THE LONGEST RAILWAY?

The world's longest railway is the Trans-Siberian Railway that runs across the Soviet Union.

The Trans-Siberian Railway was built to link European Russia with the Pacific Ocean in the Far East. The railway's name means 'across Siberia'. Its track runs right across Siberia, the northern part of Asia. This Siberian stretch of track measures 7407 kilometres from Chelyabinsk near the Ural Mountains to the port of Vladivostok on the Pacific Ocean.

You could take an even longer trip by joining the train at Moscow in European Russia. The distance from Moscow to Nakodhka, at the end of the line, is 9438 kilometres. This is the world's longest train journey. It involves 97 stops and lasts eight days.

In 1938, work started on making a short-cut to bypass a long southern loop around Lake Baikal. Laying this northern stretch of track involved shifting colossal quantities of earth and building 3700 bridges. The new line was complete by 1983. It will shorten the journey across Siberia by 500 kilometres.

▶ WHERE DID THE ORIENT EXPRESS TRAVEL?

The Orient Express was a famous luxury passenger train that used to travel across Europe from west to east and back. Its name comes from *Orient*, another word for 'east'.

The Orient Express brought great style to rail travel in Europe. The train had a library, smoking-room, ladies' boudoir, dining-car and sleeping-cars.

People sat in red-plush armchairs. They washed in bathrooms with mosaic floors and ate in a tapestry-lined dining-car with an embossed leather ceiling.

The route of the train has changed several times since the name Orient Express was first used in 1883. At times wars and other problems have made it impossible for trains to travel across all Europe.

At one time passengers could travel direct from Paris to the Turkish city of Istanbul, where Europe meets Asia. The train passed through Milan in Italy, Belgrade in Yugoslavia, and Sofia in Bulgaria. Today's nearest equivalent runs from Paris to Vienna in Austria and Bucharest in Romania.

In the early 1980s the Venice Simplon Orient Express began running between London and Venice. It brought back the luxury travel of the old-style Oriental Express.

▲ WHERE IS THE LONGEST ROAD?

The world's longest road is the Pan-American Highway. It runs from north-western North America to the far south of South America.

The Pan-American Highway extends from Alaska to Chile. In fact it is not a single road, but a system of routes linking the countries of North and Central America and those of the west coast of South America.

The highway system remains incomplete. A stretch of swampy tropical forest, called the Darién Gap, separates Panama from Colombia and so cuts off the route between Central and South America.

American nations began planning a Pan-American road link in the 1920s. They had built most of the system by the early 1950s. South American countries paid for the parts of the highway within their own borders. The United States helped to pay for the section between Texas and Panama.

▲ WHERE DO PEOPLE USE RICKSHAWS?

People use rickshaws as taxis in East and South-East Asia. They are light vehicles, often pulled or pedalled by a man, and usually carrying one passenger.

The name rickshaw comes from *jinrikisha*, which is made up of three Japanese words: *jin* (man), *riki* (power) and *sha* (vehicle).

Rickshaws were supposedly invented by a missionary to Japan in about 1870. A rickshaw has a chair-like body. It is covered with a movable hood and is mounted on springs. Early models had two large wheels with wire spokes, and two shafts. A passenger sat in the back and the rickshaw driver stood between the shafts, with which he pulled the rickshaw along. Pulling the rickshaw required great physical effort.

The use of rickshaws spread to China, India and Africa. Rickshaws with built-in cycles or motorcycle engines have mostly taken the place of the type that was pulled along.

▲ WHICH CITY HAD THE FIRST UNDERGROUND RAILWAY?

London was the world's first city to have an underground railway. The first part of this system was opened in 1863.

London needed an underground railway system by the 1860s. The city was growing fast and its streets were becoming crowded with slow, horse-drawn traffic.

Because London stands on soft clay, it was fairly easy to drive tunnels under the city. The workers dug down from street level to make the first shallow, underground track. This was built for steam trains.

Later, engineers cut new tunnels at deeper levels for railway lines served by electric passenger-trains. The London underground railway now has a number of interlinked lines that cover 410 kilometres.

Today, many cities have underground railways. They include Paris, Milan, New York and Moscow.

▼ HOW HIGH DO AIRCRAFT TRAVEL?

Different types of plane travel at a variety of altitudes, or heights. How high a plane flies depends largely on what it was designed for, and on regulations laid down by authorities that control air traffic.

Small, propeller-driven planes mostly fly at fairly low levels – high enough to avoid dangers such as mountains and tall structures, but below the flight paths that are used by jet airliners.

Jet airliners often fly at a height of about 9000 metres. *Concorde*, a supersonic airliner, flies even higher. Flying high helps planes to keep above rough weather. But air-traffic controllers assign flight levels to planes to prevent them colliding.

Some military planes can reach amazing altitudes. The American Lockheed SR-71 spy plane can fly 30.5 kilometres high, and a Russian 'Foxbat' (MiG-25) has soared to an incredible height of 37.7 kilometres.

MiG-25 'Foxbat'

▼ WHICH ARE THE WORLD'S LARGEST AIRPORTS?

In 1981 an airport at Jeddah in western Saudi Arabia became the world's largest. Two years later, Saudi Arabia completed an even larger airport, shown here in the picture, at the capital, Riyadh.

King Abdul-Aziz International Airport at Jeddah was built mainly to receive the nearly two million Muslim pilgrims who visit Mecca each year.

The airport site covers 116.6

square kilometres. There are two main runways and four terminals. The Haj terminal, the world's largest roofed building, covers 1.5 square kilometres. In style it resembles a cluster of nomads' tents, but it has marble walls and glass-fibre roofs.

In 1983, the even larger King Khaled Airport opened at Riyadh. This also has two runways and four terminals. There is a royal pavilion, as well as covered parking for 7700 cars, and buildings for the people who live and work there.

▲ WHICH ARE THE BUSIEST AIR ROUTES?

The busiest air routes are those between certain cities in North America, and over parts of Europe.

A good indication of where the most air traffic occurs is the number of people passing through different airports. Chicago International Airport handles the most flights. Nearly a quarter of a million people arrived at or left the airport in 1980. Over 43 million people passed through

it. Most were taking flights to or from other American cities.

The next busiest airport is Hartsfield International Airport at Atlanta, Georgia. A new terminal, opened in 1980, allows it to cope with up to 60 million people a year.

The busiest international airport is Heathrow Airport, London. By the early 1980s Heathrow handled more than 28 million passengers a year.

On average, more than two and a half times as many people fly in North America as in the next busiest areas: Europe and Russia.

WHERE DID THE WORST AIR ACCIDENT HAPPEN?

The worst accident in the history of air travel happened at Tenerife, one of the Canary Islands off north-west Africa. More than 500 people died when two jumbo jets collided there before take-off in 1977.

The disaster took place at Los Rodeos Airport on 27 March, 1977. The airport was crowded with planes which had been diverted there after a terrorists' bomb had exploded at a big airport on a nearby island.

A Dutch KLM Boeing-747 and a Pan-Am Boeing-747 were taxiing for take-off in mist and drizzle. The Dutch plane struck the Pan-Am plane and both burst into flames. All the 248 people aboard the Dutch plane died, and 335 perished on the other aircraft. There were over 60 survivors.

Pilot error, poor visibility and lack of radar at the airport helped to cause this terrible disaster. Nobody had noticed when one plane moved into the other's path.

WHERE CAN ENGINES BE POSITIONED IN AN AIRCRAFT?

Engineers can position aircraft engines anywhere where they will work without unbalancing the plane in flight.

All aircraft engines must be placed where pipes can feed fuel to them from storage tanks. Piston engines, turbo-jets and turbo-props must all be able to suck in air from the front and force out air or hot gases from the back, to thrust a plane forward.

Piston engines and turbo-prop engines spin airscrews (propellers) that push or pull a plane along. 'Puller' airscrews project forward from engines mounted in the nose or wings. A few planes have pusher airscrews jutting backwards from wing-mounted engines. There are even push-pull twin-engined aircraft, with airscrews at both ends.

Airliners have turbo-jets built into or slung below the wings, or on the rear fuselage. Fast warplanes have turbo-jets in or alongside the fuselage.

WHERE AND WHAT IS A 'BLACK BOX'?

The 'black box' is the popular name for a flight recorder, a device carried in aircraft. Its purpose is to reveal the cause of faults if these develop in flight.

Flight recorders show how aircraft systems behave. They give information about a plane's heading, height, air speed, rate of descent and so on. On some recorders, the information appears as lines engraved on a strip of metal foil. This is housed in a crashproof, fireproof, floatable box. In a crash the box is hurled clear and recovered later. There are also digital recorders which record the information in binary code.

Besides a flight recorder, airliners carry a cockpit voice recorder to record aircrew conversations. Between them, the flight recorder and voice recorder help experts to learn what caused a crash, even if all aboard were killed. Such information helps designers to produce safer planes.

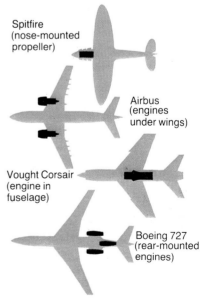

Spitfire (nose-mounted propeller)

Airbus (engines under wings)

Vought Corsair (engine in fuselage)

Boeing 727 (rear-mounted engines)

INDEX

Page numbers in *italics* refer to pictures

A
Abbas the Great 93
Abominable Snowman *see* Yeti
Aborigines 82, *82*
Abu Simbel 84, *84*
Abyssal plain 25, *25*
Acacia 50, 109
Acid rain 33
Acoushi 55
Adaptive radiation 60
Addax *39*, 53, *53*
Adélie penguin 40, *40*
Adobe 79
Aegean Sea 26, 113
Afghanistan 87
Africa *13*, *24*, *32*, 34, 79, *79*, 80, *80*, 114
African animals *39*, 43, 50, 56, 99
African pygmies *see* Negrillos
African rain forest 54, *55*
Agadir earthquake 19
Agincourt, battle of 73
Agouti 55
Agra 94
Agrippa 70
Ainu 81,*81*
Air 20, 21
Air accident 119, *119*
Airbus *119*
Aircraft 118, *118*, 119, *119*
Aircraft engine 119, *119*
Airscrew 118, 119, *119*
Air-traffic control 118
Akosombo Dam 33
Alaska 18, *18*
Alder 46
Aldrin, Edwin 103
Aleutian Islands 17, 18, *18*
Alert Bay 105
Alexander 70
Alexandria 70, 112, *112*, 115
Alhambra 91, *91*
Alice Springs 109
Ali Qapu 93
Alpaca 43
Alphabet 65
Alpine animals 42
Alps 42, 111
Amazon, river 26, 28, *28*
Amazon rain forest 35, 54, 55, 80
Ameralik Fiord 14
American colonists 75
American Indians 74, 85, 104, 105, *105*
American Revolution 75
Americas 12, 13, 35, 117
Amphibians 54
Amphitheatre 84, *84*
Amsterdam 88
Amusement park 103, *103*
Anaconda 54
Andean condor 43
Andean deer 43
Andes 16, 18, *18*, 28, 29, 36, 43
Angel, Jimmy 28
Angel Falls 28
Angkor Wat 85, *85*
Angwantibo monkey 55
Animals
  habitat 38, 39, *39*, 44, *44*, 45, *45*
  hunting 99
  national park 99

working 68, *68*, 94, *94*
Anole 54
Ant 46, *54*
Antarctica 10, *13*, 20, 22, *22*, 23, 32, 40
Antarctic Circle 10, *10*
Antarctic Circumpolar Current *see* West
  Wind Drift
Anteater 38, 49, 55
Antelope *39*, 50, 53, 55, *55*
Anticline *see* Upfold
Antipater of Sidon 112
Ape 56
Aperea *see* Pampas guinea-pig
Appalachian Mts 42
Appian Way 70
Aqua Appia 70
Aqueduct 70, *70*
Aquifer 31, *31*
Arabs 77, 79
Arab states *see* United Arab Emirates
Arch 93, *93*, 94
Archery 69, *69*, 73, *73*
Archipelago 26
Arctic Circle 10, *10*, 20, 22, *22*, 23, 41
Arctic Ocean 20, 22, 115
Arctic tern 41, 62, *62*
Arctic warbler *62*
Argali 42
Argentina 49, 106
Armadillo *38*, 49
Armenia *110*
Army 69
Armstrong, Neil 103
Arno, river 90
Arrow 69
Arrow poison frog 54
Artesian well 31, *31*
Ascension Island *32*
Ash 46
Asia 26, 34, 74, *74*, 78, *78*, 79, *114*, 117
Asian animals *39*, 46, 49, 52, 56, 57
Aspen 44
Assam 18, 19, 21, *21*
Assegais 101
Assyrians 69, *69*
Aswan High Dam 84
Atacama Desert 21
Atbara, river 28
Atlantic Ocean *13*, *13*, *24*, 26, *28*, *32*,
  113, *113*
Atlantic Ridge 12,17
Atlantis 113, *113*
Atlas Mountains 98
Atmospheric dust 17
Atomic bomb 77, *77*
Augustus 71
Australian aborigines 82, *82*, 109
Australia *13*, *26*, 37, 108, 109, *109*, *114*
Australian animals *39*, *39*, 58, 59, *59*, 61
Australian outback 109
Avalanche 16
Aven Armand cave 30
Axis 10, 11
Axle 65
Ayers Rock 109, *109*
Azerbaijan *110*
Azores 17

B
Baboon 55
Babylon 112, *112*
Bactrian camel *39*, 52, *52*

Baden-Baden 88
Baden-Württemberg 88
Badger 46, *47*, 48, *48*
Bahrain 21
Baikal, lake 116
Bald eagle 42
Bali tiger *56*
Baltic Sea 115
Bamboo 43
Bamian 87
Banded mongoose 51
Bandicoot 59
Bangkok 95
Bangladesh 93, *93*
Banksia 58, *58*
Bank vole 46
Baobab tree 50
Barbarians 71, 89
Barge 79, 114
Barter 67
Bartholdi, Frédéric-Auguste 102
Basalt 37
Bat-eared fox 51
Baths 70
Bathurst Island 10
Bathyscaphe 25
Bay of Fundy 26
Bear 45
Beaver 42
Bedouin 78, *78*
Beech 46, 88
Beech marten 46
Beehive mud house 79
Beetle 46, 53, 54
Beijing 97, *97*
Belgium 88, 96
Bellbird 54
Bellows 69
Bell tower 90
Benares *see* Varanasi
Bengal, Bay of 93
Bengal tiger *56*
Benin 100
Berbers 82, 98
Bergschrund 23
Bering Strait 74, *74*
Bermuda Triangle 113, *113*
Bharal 42
Biafo Glacier 22
Bible 71
Big game 99
Big Hole 33
Bighorn sheep 42, *42*
Bingham, Hiram 85
Bingham Canyon Copper Mine 33, *33*
Biome 38, 54
Birch 44, 46
Bird-eating spider *54*
Birds 42, *42*, 46, 52, 53
  flightless 61, *61*
  migration 62, *62*
  national park 99
  pampas 50. *51*
  rain forest 54, *54*
Birds of paradise 58, *58*
Birds of prey 42, 46, 50
Bison 48, *48*
Black bear 45
Blackbird 46
Black box 119
Black-footed ferret 48
Black Forest 88, *88*

Black Hills 104
Black rhinoceros 56
Black Sea 29, 92
Black spruce 44
Blackthorn 46
Black Volta 33
Black vulture 42
Bluebell 46
Blue jay 46, 47
Blue Nile, river 28, 28
Blue tit 46, 47
Blue whale 62
Boa constrictor 54
Boar 46
Boat-dwellers 79, 79
Bobcat 38, 46, 47, 52
Bobolink 62
Boeing aircraft 119, 119
Boiling mud 19
Bola 106
Bolivia 106
Bolt 68
Bombay 93
Bongo 55, 55
Bon-seki garden 97
Booby 60
Book 65, 73, 73
Boomerang 82
Bore see Tidal bore
Boreal forest 44
Borglum, Gutzon 104
Borneo 57
Bosporus 92
Boston Tea Party 75
Bouvet Island 32
Boxer Rebellion 75, 76, 76
Boyoma Falls 101
Brahmaputra, river 93
Brasilia 107, 107
Bratsk Reservoir 33
Brazil 107
Brent goose 41, 41
Brian Head 14
Bridge 70, 90, 90, 108, 108, 110, 110, 116
British colonies 75
Broadway 102
Bromeliads 43
Bronze 69
Bronze Age 79
Brown bear 44, 45
Brown hare 39
Bryce Canyon 14
Buddha 87, 87, 94
Buddhists 94, 95
Buenos Aires 32
Bulbul 50
Burrowing owl 49, 52, 52
Bushbaby 55
Bushmen 80, 80
Bustard 50
Butte 36
Butterfly 53, 54, 63, 63
Buzzard 46
Byelorussia 110
Byzantium 92
Byzas 92

C
Cacao tree 35, 35
Cactus 52
Cactus wren 52, 52
Caecus, Appius Claudius 70
Cairo 21
Calcite 15
Calcium carbonate 30
Caldera 37
California 13
California grey whale 62
Cambodia see Kampuchea
Camel 52, 52
Camel caravans 98
Camouflage 54
Canadian lynx 42

Canadian Shield 14
Canal 70, 88, 88, 89, 95, 95, 100, 100, 103, 114
Canal do Norte 26, 28
Canary Islands 119
Canyon 14
Capercaillie 45
Cape Canaveral 103, 103
Cape Town 32
Capuchin 55
Carbon 15
Carbonic acid 33
Cargo 114
Caribou 38, 41, 41, 45
Carnival 107, 107
Carnivores 41, 45, 46, 59
Carpathian Mts 42
Carrao, river 28
Carrion-eaters 42
Cart 65, 67
Caspian Sea 29, 29
Caspian tiger 56
Carving 84, 85, 104
Cassowary 61, 61
Casting 100, 100
Castle 92
Cathay 72
Cathedral 89, 89, 91
Cattle ranch 106, 109
Cave 30, 30
Cave dwelling 87
Cave painting 109
Cavy 49
Central Africa 83
Central America 18, 18, 35, 85, 85, 104, 117
Central Asia 78
Central Asian desert 52
Central heating 70
Central Park 102
Cereals 34, 35
Chaffinch 46
Chain-mail 69
Chalet 78
Chalk 31
Challenger (survey ship) 25
Challenger Deep 25
Chamois 42
Chao Phraya, river 95
Chartres cathedral 89, 89
Cheetah 50, 51
Chelyabinsk 116
Cherrapunji 21
Cherun-Meru see Angel Falls
Chevrotain 55
Chicago 111, 111
Chickaree 44, 45
Ch'ient'ang'kian, river 26
Chile 18, 18, 106
Chilean pine 43
Chimpanzee 39, 55, 55
China 18 18, 26, 29, 75, 75, 76, 76, 79, 79, 97
    ancient 65, 69, 69, 72, 73
Chinese pagoda 95, 95
Chinese tiger 56
Chinstrap penguin 40, 40
Chipmunk 44, 45, 46, 47
Chocolate 35
Chough 42
Christ see Jesus
Christianity 72, 86, 87, 92, 99
Christ the Redeemer (statue) 107
Church 86, 87, 99, 99
Civet 51
City-state 67, 70
Civilization 64
Civil War (US) 76
Clay pot 66
Clay tablet 65, 65
Cliff dwellings 87, 105, 105
Climate 20–21, 20–21, 38, 38
Cloven-hoofed animals 42
Coati monkey 55

Cockpit voice recorder 119
Cocoa 35, 35
Cocoon 66
Coin 67, 67
Cold 20, 20, 21
Cold current 24, 24
Collared anteater 55
Colobus monkey 55, 55
Colombia 18, 117
Colorado Desert 14
Colorado Plateau 36, 36
Colorado river 14
Colosseum 84, 84
Colossus 84, 112, 112
Colour (regimental flag) 89
Colour marking 54
Colugo see Flying lemur
Columbus 73, 74, 74
Column-like rock 36, 37
Compass 10
Concorde 118
Condor 43
Conduit 70
Conglomerate 15
Coniferous forest 38, 38, 43, 44–45, 44–45
Constantine, emperor 92
Constantinople 71, 92
Container vessel 114
Constructive plate margin 12, 12
Continent 13
Continental plate 12
Continental shelf 25, 25
Copper 69
Coral reef 27
Coral snake 54
Cormorant 60, 60
Corcovado 107
Corn see Maize
Cornflakes 35
Costa, Lucio 107
Coterie 48
Cotinga 54, 54
Cotton 34, 34
Cotton boll 34
Cottontail 52, 52
Coubertin, Pierre de 66
Cougar see Mountain lion
Count Raggi's bird of paradise 58
Cow 106, 106
Cowboy 106
Coyote 48, 48
Coypu 38
Crab 61, 61
Crabeater seal 40, 40
Crab-eating macaque 57
Crab-eating racoon 55
Crane 50
Creac'h d'Ouessant lighthouse 115
Crevasse 23, 23
Cricket 53, 54
Crossbill 45
Crown of Thorns starfish 27
Crowther, Mrs P. 30
Crusades 92
Crust 12, 12, 13, 14
Crustal plate 12, 12
Crystals 15
Cuckoo 62
Cueva de Nerja 30
Cuneiform script 65
Curassow 54, 54
Curlew 52
Current see Ocean current
Cuscus 59

D
Dam 32, 33
Danube, river 88
Darién Gap 117
Darwin's finches 60
Dasyure 59
Date 100
Date Line 11, 11

Dating 14
Dead Sea *13*, 25
Dead Sea Scrolls 71, *71*
Death Valley 20, *20*, 52
De Brazza monkey 55
Deciduous forest 38, *38*, 44, 46, *47*
Declaration of Independence 102
Deep-sea trench *see* Ocean trench
Deer *38*, *39*, 43, 46, *47*, 49
de Lesseps, Ferdinand 100
Delta 93
Delta Project 32
Desert 20, *20*, 21, 29, 31, 36, 38, *38*, 53,
    59, 100, *100*, 109
Desert animals 52, *52*, 53, *53*
Desert-dwellers 78, *78*
Desert plants 52
Destructive plate margin 12
Dew 20
Dew claw 42
Dey 98
Diamond 15, *15*, 33
Diamondback rattlesnake 52
Diamond Sutra (book) 73, *73*
Diana monkey 55
Digital recorder 119
Dikdik 51
Dingo *39*
Disney, Walt 103
Disneyland 103, *103*
Display 58
Dodo 61
Dog's mercury 46
Doldrums 24, *24*
Dome 86, *86*, 90, 93, *93*, 94, *94*, 95
Dome of the Rock 86, *86*
Don, river *29*
Door lock 68, *68*
Dormouse *39*, 46, *47*
Douroucoulis 55
Drainage ditch 32
Drake Passage 24
Drill 55
Dry climate 21, 38, *38*, 109
Duck 41, 43
Duiker 55
Dune *see* Sand dune
Dunlin 41
Dusky langur 57
Dust bowl 31
Dyke 29, 32

E
Eagle 42, *42*, *54*
Eared agama *52*
Ear 53
Earth
    axis 10, *10*, 11
    crust 12, 14
    movements 13
Earthquake 12, 13, 18, *18*, 19
East Africa 34, 36
East Asia 79, 81
Easter Island 112, *112*
Eastern chipmunk *47*
Eastern Roman Empire 71, 92
East Indies 73
East Pakistan 93
East River 102
Echo-sounding 25
Ecuadorian pudu 43
Edo 96
Education 71
Eel 63, *63*
Egypt *13*, 34
    ancient 68, 69, 84, *84*, 112, *112*, 115
Eland 51, 53, *53*
Elder 46
El Dorado 74, *74*
Electric train 117
Elephant *50*, 51, 94, *94*, 99, *99*
Elephant bird 61
Elephant shrew *55*
Elf owl 52

Elk 45
Emperor penguin 40, *40*
Empty Quarter, The *see* Rub'-al-Khali
Emu 61, *61*
Engine 119, *119*
English Channel 114
Ephesus 112, *112*
Epicentre 19, *19*
Equator 10, 20, 24, *24*, *28*, *32*, 36, 38, 54
Erg 53
Erosion 31, 33, *33*, 36, 37
Escorial 90, *90*
Eskimos 83, *83*
Estonia *110*
Estuary 26
Ethiopia 99
Eucalyptus 58, *59*, 109
Eurasia 13, *13*, 16, 20
Eurasian taiga 44, 45
Europe 24, *24*, 34, *39*, 42, 44, 46, *114*
Everest, George 16
Everest, Mount 16, *16*, 81
Evolution 60
Exchanging goods *see* Barter
Extinct birds 61
Eyre highway 108

F
Fairweather fault 13
Fairy armadillo 49
Falcon 41, 50, *53*
Fallow deer 46, *47*
Farming 31, 64, *64*, 68, *68*
Faulting 12, 13, 19, 36
Feldberg 88
Feldspar 15
Fennec *39*, 53, *53*
Fern 54
Ferret 48
Fieldfare 41
Field maple 46
Fifth Avenue 102
Finch 43, 60, *60*
Fingal's Cave 37
Fiord 27
Fir 44, *45*, 88
Fire 44, 49
Fireworks 69
Fish 52
Fishing boat 29
Flesh-eating animals *see* Carnivores
Flight 118, 119
Flightless birds 60, 61, *61*
Flight recorder *see* Black Box
Flint Ridge Caves 30
Flood 29, 32, 33
Florence 90, *90*
Flour 35
Flycatcher 46
Flying frog 56
Flying lemur *39*, 56, *56*
Flying lizard 56
Flying phalanger 59
Flying squirrel 44, 45, 56
Focus 19, *19*
Fog-warning 115
Fold mountain *12*
Forbidden City 97, *97*
Foremast light 115
Forest 38, *38*, 44–45, *44–45*, 46, *47*, 57,
    57
Forest fire 44
Fortress 91, 92, 98
Fossil 14
Fox 41, 46, *47*, 51, *52*
Foxbat aircraft 118
French Revolution 89
Frigatebird 60, *60*
Frog 54
Frost 20, *20*
Fungus 54

G
Galago monkey 55
Galapagos animals 60, *60*
Gall wasp *47*
Ganges, river 87, 93
Gao 74
Garden 97, *97*, 104, *104*, 112, *112*
Gases 33
Gaucho 106, *106*
Gaza 77
Gazelle 50, 51, 52
Gemsbok *39*
Genet *55*
Gentoo penguin 40, *40*
Georgia, USSR 34, *110*
Ger *see* Yurt
Gerbil 53
Gerenuk *50*
Geyser 37, *37*
Ghats 87
Giant anteater 49
Giant armadillo 49
Giant forest hog 55
Giant lobelia 43
Giant lupin 43, *43*
Giant panda 43, *43*
Giant puya 43
Giant's Causeway 37, *37*
Giant tortoise 60
Gibbon 56
Gila monster 52
Ginza 96, *96*
Giraffe *39*, *50*, 51
Glacial lake 29
Glacier 16, 22, 23, *23*, 27, 28
Gladiator 84
Glazing 66
Gliding snake 56
Gneiss 14
Goat 42
Goat-antelope 42, 43
Gobi Desert 21, 52, 100
Gold 15, *15*
Gold and blue macaw *54*
Golden chipmunk 45
Golden eagle 42, *42*
Golden mole *39*
Golden Pagoda 94, *94*
Golden plover *62*
Golden Temple 87
Goldfinch 46
Gold-hooded manakin *54*
Gold rush 15
Goosander *45*
Goose 41, *41*
Goral 43
Gorilla 55, *55*
Gothic style 89, *89*
Goths 89
Gouffre de la Pierre Saint-Martin 30
Granada 91
Grand Canyon 14, *14*
Grand Erg Oriental 31
Grand Trianon 89
Granite 15, 37
Granite Gorge 14
Grant's gazelle 51, *51*
Grasshopper 53
Grasshopper mouse 52
Grassland 38, *38*, 49, 50–51, *50–51*, *59*
Grazing animals 49, 50, 51
Great Artesian Basin 31
Great Barrier Reef 27
Great curassow *54*
Greater bird of paradise *58*
Greater shearwater 62, *62*
Greater spotted woodpecker *47*
Great horned owl 44
Great Lakes 29, 103, 115
Great Rift Valley 13
Great tit 46
Great Zimbabwe 101, *101*
Greece, ancient 66, *66*, 67, *67*, 70, 112,
    112

Green iguana 54
Greenland 14, 22, *22*, 23, 32
Green turtle 63, *63*
Greenwich Meridian 10, *10*, 11
Green woodpecker *47*
Grey fox 46, *47*
Grey kangaroo 59
Grey monitor *52*
Grey squirrel 45, 46, *47*
Grey whale 62, *62*
Grey wolf 48
Griffon 42
Griffon vulture *50*
Ground hornbill 50
Groundsel 43, *43*
Ground squirrel 42, *44*, 45
Guadarrama Mts 90
Guanaco 43, 49, *49*
Guardsman 89
Guemel 43
Guenon 55
Guinea-pig 49
Gulf Stream 24, *24*
Gunpowder 69
Gutenberg, Johannes 73
Gypsy 81, *81*
Gyr falcon 41

H
Habitat 38–39, *38–39*, 44–45, *44–45*, 54
Hadrian 84
Hairy armadillo 49, *49*
Halemaumau, lake 16
Halicarnassus, Mausoleum of 112, *112*
Hamada 53
Hamlyn's monkey 55
Hanging Gardens of Babylon 112, *112*
Harbour 114, 115
Hare *39*, *45*, 49
Harlem River 102
Harpy eagle 54, *54*
Hartebeest 50
Hawaii 16, 17, 18, *18*, 21, 60
Hawfinch 46
Hawk 52
Hazel 46
Hazel hen *45*
Head carving 104, *104*, 112, *112*
Healing centre 19
Heat 20, *20*, 21
Heating 70
Hedgehog *39*, 46, *47*, 52
Hegira 72
Hemignathus procerus 60
Herbaceous plants 44, 46, 49
Herbivores 41, 45, 46, 48, 49, 51, 52, 53
Herculaneum 18
Herd 50
Hickory 46
High Andes 43
High Dam 84
High-mountain vole 42
Hillary, Edmund 81
Himalaya-Karakoram Range 16, 22, 81, *81*, 113
Himalayan animals 42
Hindu Kush Mountains 87
Hindus 87, *87*
Hippopotamus *39*
Hippo's Yawn 37
Hiroshima 77
Hispar glacier 22
Hoary marmot 42
Hoatzin 54
Hog 55
Hokkaido 81
Holly 46
Holy City 86, 87
Holy Sepulchre, Church of the 86
Honeycreeper 54, 60, *60*
Honeyeater 58
Honey possum 58, *58*
Honeysuckle 46

Hong Kong 75, 79, *79*
Honshu 96
Hooghly, river 26
Hooved animals 42, 50, 55, 59
Horizon 11
Hornbeam 46
Hornbill 50, 54
Horned frog 54
Horned viper 53
Horse 68, 74, *106*
Horse chestnut 46
Horse Guards Parade 89
Hot spring 37
House 70, 78, *78*, 79, *79*, 83, 98
Houseboat 79
Household Brigade of Guards 89
Howler monkey *54*, 55
Hudson River 102
Hull 115
Humber Estuary Bridge 110, *110*
Hummingbird 54, *54*
Humpback whale 62
Humps, The 37
Humus 44, 46
Hwang-ho, river 29
Hyden Rocks 37
Hydro-electric power 33
Hyena 51
Hypocaust 70, *70*

I
Ibex 42, *42*
Ice 20
Iceberg 23, *23*
Icebreaker 115, *115*
Ice cap *22*
Iceland 17, 22, *22*
Ice sheet 22, 23
Igloo 83
Igneous rock 15
Iguana 60, *60*
Ijssel, lake 32
Imperial Palace 96
Impervious rock 31, *31*
Impis 101
Incas 85, *85*
India 18, 34, 93
Indian Ocean *28*, 113
Indian Plate 16
Indian rhinoceros *56*
Indians *see* American Indians
Indies 73, 74
Indochinese tiger *56*
Indonesia 17, 26, *26*, 34, 35, 114, *114*
Insects 53, 54
International Date Line 11, *11*
Invertebrates 46
Iran *29*, 114, *114*
Iron 69
Irrigation 29, 31, 68
Isaouane-n-Tifernine 31
Isfahan 93, *93*
Islam 72, 86
Island 17, 18, 25, 26, 32
Island animals 60, *60*, 61, *61*
Island arc *12*, 26
Israel 77, 86
Istanbul 92, *92*, 116
Isthmus of Suez 100

J
Jacamar 54, *54*
Jackal *50*, 51
Jack rabbit 42
Jaguar 55
Japan 18, *18*, 34, 77, 81, *114*
   customs 96, *96*, 97, *97*
Japura, river *28*
Javan rhinoceros 56, *56*
Java Trench 26
Jay 46, *47*
Jefferson, Thomas *104*
Jerboa *39*, 52, *52*, 53
Jerusalem 86, *86*

Jesus 86
Jet airline 118, 119, *119*
Jews 77, 86
John F. Kennedy Space Center 103
Jostedal Glacier 28
Judaism 86
Jumbo jet 119, *119*
Jute 93

K
Kagera, river *28*
Kaibab Limestone 14
Kalahari Desert 80
Kamchatka Peninsula 18, *18*
Kampuchea 85
Kanamori scale 18
Kangaroo *39*, 59, *59*
Kangaroo rat *38*, 52, *52*
Kasbah 98, *98*
Kayak 83
Kazakhstan *110*
Keihin Metropolitan Area 96
Kenya 99
Khmers 85
Khumba Valley 81
Kiev *110*
Kilauea Crater 16
Kilimanjaro, Mount 36, *36*
Kimberley mine 33
Kimberlite 15, 33
King penguin 40
King Rocks 37
Kinkajou 55
Kirgizia *110*
Kite 46
Kit fox 52, *52*
Kivas 105
Kiwi 61, *61*
Klongs 95, *95*
Knights Hospitallers 92
Knot 41
Koala *39*, 59, *59*
Koran 72, 91
Kori bustard 50
Kraal 101
Krakatoa Island 17, *17*
Krak des Chevaliers 92, *92*
Kremlin 91, *91*
Kublai Khan 72
Kudu 51
Kurile Islands 81
Kwakiutl Indians 105
KwaZulu 101

L
Labrador Current 23
Lacewing *47*
Laetoli 64
La Grande Stalagmite 30
Lake 13, *13*, 29, *29*, 36; artificial 33, *33*
Lalibela 99
Lamb 108
Lambert-Fisher Ice Passage 22
Lammergeier vulture 42, *42*
Land
   bridge 74, *74*
   mass 13
   reclamation 32, *32*, 88
Langur 56, 57, *57*
Lanner falcon 50, *53*
La Paz 106, *106*
Lapland 83
Lapps 83, *83*
Larch 44, *44*
Lark 52, 53
Latex 35
Latin 71
Latvia *110*
Launching site, 103, *103*
Lava 12, 16
Leafcutter ant *54*
Leaning Tower 90, *90*
Lebatine viper 52

Lebu earthquake 18
Leipzig, battle of 69
Lemming *45*
Lenin Mausoleum 91, *91*
Leningrad *110*
Leopard 51
Leopard seal 40, *40*
Lesseps, Ferdinand de *see* de Lesseps
Lesser panda *see* Red panda
Lhasa 97
Liana 54
Liberia 76
Libya 114, *114*
Lighthouse 112, *112*, 115, *115*
Limestone 14, 33
Lincoln, Abraham *104*
Lion 38, *39*, 51, *51*
Lithuania *110*
Little king bird of paradise 58
Livingstone, David 101
Lizard 52, *52*, 53, 54
Llama 29, *38*, 43, *43*
Lobelia 43
Lock
    canal 103
    door 68, *68*
Lockheed aircraft 118
Locust 53
Lodgepole pine 44, *44*
Log cabin 78
London 89, 117
Longbow 73, *73*
Long-eared hedgehog 52
Longitude 10
Long-legged maned wolf 49, *49*
Long-tailed duck 41
Long-tailed weasel 46
Loom *105*
Loris 56
Los Rodeos Airport 119
Louis XIV, French king 89
Lourdes 87, *87*
Lovely cotinga *54*
Low Countries 88, *88*
Lupin 43, *43*
Luxembourg 88
Lynx *39*, 42, 46

M
Maas, river *see* Meuse, river
Macaque 56, 57
Macaroni penguin 40, *40*
Macaw 54, *54*
MacCool, Finn 37
Macedonia 70
Machu Picchu 85, *85*
Mackinac Straits Bridge 110
Madagascar 34
Madeira, river *28*
Magellan, Ferdinand 106
Magellan, Strait of 106
Magnetic field 10
Magnetic North Pole 10, *10*
Magnolia 46
Mahout 94
Mainmast 115
Maize 35
Malawi, lake 13, *13*
Malaysia 26, *26*, 35
Mali 98
Mammals 39, 41, 52, 55, *55*
Mammoth Cave National Park 30, *30*
Manakin 54, *54*
Maned wolf 49, *49*
Mangrove forest 57, *57*
Manhattan 102, *102*
Mantis 54
Mantle 12, *12*
Manx shearwater 62
Maoris 82, *82*
Maple 46
Mara 49, *49*
Marabou stork 50
Marajo Island *28*

Marco Polo *see* Polo, Marco
Margay cat 55
Mariana Trench 25
Markhor 42, *42*
Marmoset *38*, *54*, 55
Marmot 42, *42*
Marsupials 59, *59*
Marten 46
Marunouchi district 96
Mary Rose 73
Masai 80, *80*
Masthead light 115
Mauna Kea 16
Mauna Loa 16
Mausoleum 94, *94*, 112, *112*
Mayflower 75, *75*
Mausolus, king 112, *112*
Maze 89
Mecca 72
Medical school 71
Medieval period *see* Middle Ages
Medina 72
Mediterranean Sea 92, 100
Meridian 10, 11
Melanesia 109
Merino sheep 108
Mesa Verde 105, *105*
Mesopotamia 68
Meuse, river 32
Mexico 104
Mexico City, 96, 104, *104*
Micronesia 109
Middle Ages 69, 72, 73, 92, *92*
Midnight sun 10
Mid-ocean ridge 12, *12*
Migration 50, 62, *62*
Military aircraft 118
Minaret 94
Mindanao 80
Mining 33
Mink *44*, 45
Missile 69, 103
Mississippi-Missouri, rivers 28
Mist 20
Moa 61
Mobutu, lake 13, *13*
Moguls 94
Mole 59
Moldavia *110*
Mole shrew 43
Monarch butterfly 63, *63*
Money 67, *67*
Mongolian gazelle 52
Mongoose *39*, 51
Monitor *52*
Monkey *38*, *39*, *54*, 55, *55*, 56, 57, *57*
Monkey puzzle tree 43, *43*
Monroe, James 76
Monrovia 76
Monsoon 21
Monument Valley 36, *36*
Moon landing 103
Moors 72, *72*, 91
Moose *44*, 45
Moroccans 74
Moscow 91, *91*, 110, *110*, 116
Moskva, river 91
Mosque 93, *93*, 94
Moss 46, 54
Moth *47*, 53
Mouflon 42
Mouhot, Henri 85
Mountain 12, 16, 38, *38*
Mountain animals 42, *42*, 43, *43*
Mountain beaver *38*
Mountain plants 43
Mount Rushmore National Memorial 104, *104*
Mount St Helens 12
Mouse 46, 52, 59
Moustached monkey 55
Mudflat 57
Mud hut 79, *79*, 80

Mud pool 19
Mudskipper *57*
Muhammad 72, 86
Mule deer 42
Murray-Darling, river 28
Musk oxen 41
Muslims 72, 82, 86, 92, 93, 98
Mutton 108

N
Nagasaki 77
Nakodhka 116
Nanking, Treaty of 75
Nam Tso, lake 29
Naples 18
NASA *see* National Aeronautics and
    Space Administration
Natal 101
National Aeronautics and Space
    Administration (NASA) 103
National park 99, 105, *105*
Navaho Indians 105, *105*
Nave 89
Navigation lights 115
Negrillos 83, *83*
Negro 100, 101
Negro, river *28*
Nepal 81, *81*
Nero 84
Netherlands 32, 88, 114
New Guinea 58, 80
New Orleans 107
New Rome 92
New South Wales 108
New Waterway canal 114
New World monkey 55
New York 102, *102*
New Zealand 61, 82
Ngorongoro Crater 99
Nice 107
Niemeyer, Oscar 107
Nieuwe Maas 114
Niger, river 98
Nigeria 79
Nightingale 46
Nightjar 46
Night lizard *52*
Nile, river 28, 84, 100
Nine-banded armadillo 49
Nitric acid 33
Nomads 78, *78*, 82, *82*, 98
Nordwest Fiord 27
Norgay, Tenzing 81
North Africa 53, 72, 98, *98*
North America 12, 13, *13*, 14, *24*, 74, *74*,
    75, *75*, 100, 114, 117
North American animals *39*, 42, 44, *44*,
    45, 46, 52
North American Indians 105, *105*
North American prairies 48, 49
North-East Trade Winds 21, 24
Northern lynx *39*, 45
Northern Territory 109
North Island 19
North Pole 10, *10*, 22, 36, 38
North Sea 114
Norway 27, 32
Norway spruce 44
Nuba 79
Nullabor Plain 108, *108*
Numbat 59

O
Oak, 46, 88
Oases 100, *100*
Oba 100
Ocean 13, 16
Ocean current 24
Ocean floor 12, 14, 25, *25*
Ocean trench 12, 17, 18, 25, *25*, 26
Ocelot 55
Oil 35, 92
    rig *92*

sea-routes 114
tanker 114
Ojos del Salada 16
Okapi 55, *55*
Old Faithful 37, *37*
Old Testament 71
Olduvai Gorge 64
Old World Monkeys 55
Olmecs 104, *104*
Olympia 112, *112*
Olympic Games 66, *66*, 112
Omnivorous birds 46, 62
One Hundred Years War 73
Open mining 33
Opera house 108, *108*
Opium War 75, *75*
Opossum 45, 59
Orang-utan *39*, 56, 57, *57*
Orient Express 116, *116*
Oriole *52*
Oryx 53
Osprey 42
Ostrich 50, *51*
Outback 109
Ouzel 42, *42*
Owl *44*, *45*, 46, 49, 52, *52*
Ox 68, *68*
Oxpecker 50, *50*

P
Pacific Ocean 13, *13*, 16, 17, 18, *18*, 25, *114*
Pacific Ocean islands 81, 109
Pacific Plate 12, 13, 18
Pacific Rim 42
Pack ice *22*, 40, 41
Paddyfield 34
Pagoda 94, *94*, 95, *95*
Pakistan 34, 93
Palace 86, *86*, 89, *89*, 90, 91, 97
Palace fortress 91
Palestine 71, 77
Pampas 49, *49*, 106
Pampas cat 49
Pampas deer 49, *49*
Pampas guinea-pig 49
Panama Canal *114*
Pan-Am Boeing aircraft 119, *119*
Pan-American Highway 117, *117*
Panda *39*, 43, *43*
Pangea 13
Pangolin *55*
Panning 15, *15*
Panthalassa 13
Paper 65
Paper money 67
Papua-New Guinea 18, *18*, 26, *26*
Papyrus 65
Parade 89, 91
Paradise jacamar *54*
Parakeet 58
Parchment 65
Parrot 54
Partridge 42
Passenger train 116, *116*
Patagonian hare *see* Mara
Patagonian steppe 49
Paving 67
Peccary *38*
Peking 96, 97
Peking, siege of 76
Penguin 40, *40*, 60
Pennsylvania Avenue 102
Peregrine falcon 41
Permafrost *22*, *22*
Persia 93
Persian Gulf 92, *114*
Petit Trianon 89
Petermann's Glacier 22
Petrel *see* Shearwater
Phalanger 59
Phalarope 41
Pharaoh 112

Philip II, Spanish king 90
Philippines 26, *26*, 79
Phoenicians 65
Picture writing 65, 112
Pika 42
Pile dwellings 78, *78*
Pilgrimage 87, *87*, 94
Pilgrim Fathers 75, *75*
Pine 43, 44, *45*
Pine marten 46
Pine vole 46
Pintail sandgrouse *53*
Pipit *62*
Pisa 90, *90*
Pisa, cathedral of 90
Piston engine 119
Pitcairn Island 112
Pit house 105
Pitti Palace 90
Placer deposit 15
Plains 108, 109
Plains bison 48
Plane *see* Aircraft
Plane tree 46
Plant-eating animals *see* Herbivores
Plants 38, 43, 44, 46
Plate boundary *18*
Plates 12, *12*, 16
Plato 113
Platypus *39*
Plaza of Three Powers 107
Plough 68, *68*
Plover *62*
Polar bear 41, *41*
Polar regions *see* North Pole, South Pole
Polder 32
Polecat 46
Pollination 58, *58*
Pollution 33
Polo, Marco 72, *72*
Polo brothers 72
Polynesia 109
Polynesians 109, 112
Polyp 27
Pompeii *18*, *18*
Ponte Vecchio 90, *90*
Poopo, lake 29
Poor-will 52
Pope 86, 111
Population 32, 97
Porcupine 45
Porous rock 31, *31*
Port 114, 115
Port light 115
Port Said 100
Port side *115*
Potlatch 105
Potter's wheel 66, *66*
Pottery 66, *66*
Potto monkey 55
Pouched mammals *see* Marsupials
Power station 26
Prairie animals 48, *48*
Prairie dog 48, *48*
Prairie wolf *see* Coyote
Predatory animals 45, 46, 48, 49, 51, 52, 55
Prehensile tail 55
President (USA) 102
Pretty-faced wallaby *59*
Pride 51
Prime Meridian 10
Primitive man 64, *64*, 65, 69
Primrose 46
Printing press 65, 73
Prison settlement 108
Proboscis monkey 57, *57*
Pronghorn *38*, 48, *48*, 52
Propeller *see* Airscrew
Psitirostra cantans 60
Pudu 43
Puffbird 54, *54*
Pupfish 52, *52*
Purus, river *28*

Puya raymondii 43
Pygmies 83, *83*
Pyramid 85, *85*, 112, *112*
Pyrenean desman 42
Pyrenees 42

Q
Quarayaq glacier 22
Quarry 33
Quartz 15, 24
Quebec *103*
Quelea 50
Quoll 59

R
Rabbit 42, 46, *47*, 59
Racoon 46, *47*, 55
Rail bird 61
Railway 108, 116, *116*, 117, *117*
Rain 21, *21*, *31*, 33, 49
Rain forest 35, 38, *38*, 54, *54*, 55, *55*, 57
Ramses II 84
Rance estuary 26
Rangoon 94
Rat *52*, 53, 61
Rat kangaroo 59
Rattlesnake 52, *52*
Raven 41, 42
Reclamation 32, *32*, 88
Recorder 119
Red bird of paradise *58*
Red-eyed vireo *47*
Red fox 46, *47*
Red-headed turkey vulture 42, *42*
Red-headed woodpecker *47*
Red kangaroo 59
Red-mantled tamarin *54*
Red oat-grass 50
Red panda 43, *43*
Redpoll 41
Red Sea 13, *13*, *28*, 100
Red Square 91, *91*
Red squirrel *39*, 45, 46
Red-throated pipit *62*
Reed 29
Reef 27, 115
Reg 53
Regiment 89
Reindeer 41
Reindeer moss 41
Religion 72, 86, 87
Reptiles 54
Reservations (Reserves) 105, *105*
Reservoir 32, 33
Rhea 49, *49*
Rhine, river 32, 88, 114
Rhinoceros 51, 56, *56*
Rice 34, *34*, 93, 100
Richter, Charles 18
Richter scale 18
Rickshaw 117, *117*
Rift valley 13
Ring ouzel 42, *42*
Ring-tailed cat 46
Rio de Janeiro 32, 107
Rio Para 28, *28*
River 26, 28, *28*, 36
Road 67, *67*, 117, *117*
Road tunnel 111, *111*
Roaring Forties 24
Robber crab 61, *61*
Rock 14, *14*, 15, 31, *31*, 36, *36*, 109, *109*
Rocket 69, *69*, 103, 108
Rockhopper penguin 40
Rock ptarmigan 41, *41*
Rock strata 14, *14*
Rocky Mountain goat *38*, 42, *42*
Rocky Mts 42
Rodent 49, 52, 53, 55, 59
Roe deer *39*, 46, *47*
Roman Catholic Church 86, 87
Romanesque style 90, *90*
Romans 18, 65; 67, 70, *70*, 71, *71*, 84, *84*
Romany 81

Rome 86, *86*, 111, *111*
Rongorongo script 112
Roof 78, 79
Rookery 40
Roosevelt, Theodore *104*
Ross, James Clark 10
Ross Ice Shelf 23
Ross seal 40
Rotterdam *114*
Rotterdam-Europoort 114
Royal antelope *55*
Royal Observatory, Greenwich 10
Royal Square 93, *93*
Rub'-al-Khali 31
Rubber 35, *35*, 104
Rubythroat *45*
Rufous ovenbird 49, *49*
Rushmore, Mount 104
Russia 110, *110*

S
Safari 99
Saguaro cactus 52
Sahara Desert 20, 31, 53, 98. 100
Saiga antelope *39*
St Basil's Cathedral 91, *91*
St Gotthard Massif 111
St Gothard Rail Tunnel 111
St Gothard Road Tunnel 111, *111*
St Helena 32, *32*
St Helens, Mount *see* Mount St Helens
St Lawrence River 103
St Lawrence Seaway 103, *103*
St Lucia Island 19
St Peter 86
St Peter's Basilica 86, *86*, 111
St Pious X, Basilica of 87
Sakhalin Island 81
Saki monkey 55
Salt 25, *25*
Saltbush 108
Salt crystal 15
Sampan 79
San Andreas fault 13
Sand dune 31, *31*, 53
Sandfish 53
Sandgrouse 52, 53, *53*
Sand rat 53, *53*
Sand-sea 31
Sandstone 14, 36, 109
San Francisco 13, *13*, 18
San Juan de Fuca Plate 12
Sanskrit 16
Santorini 113, *113*
Sarawak 30
Sarawak Chamber 30
Satellite 103
Saudi Arabia 31, 114, *114*
Savannah 50
Scarlet tanager *47*
Scarp 13
Scheldt, river 32
Scorpion 53
Scotland 37
Scots pine 44
Scott's oriole 52, *52*
Scroll 71, *71*
Scrub *59*
Sculpture 84, 87, 99, 104, *104*
Sea *see* Ocean
Sea-floor spreading 12
Seal 40, *40*
Sea lanes 114, *114*
Sea level *11*, 25
Sea-mount 25
Sea mountain 16, 25
Sears, Roebuck and Company 111
Sears Tower 111, *111*
Sea salt 25
Seaway 100, *100*, 103, *103*
Secretary bird 50
Sedimentary rock 36
Seed-eating animals 45, 62
Seismic waves 19, *19*

Semi-desert 31
Sens 89
Serengeti National Park 51, 99
Serow 43, 113
Serval 51
Seven Wonders of the World 112, *112*
Seville 72
Shah Jahan 94
Shaka 101
Shale 14
Shearwater 62
Sheep 108, *108*, 109
Sherpa 81, *81*
Sidelights 115
Shield 69
Shingle 78
Ship canal 100, *100*
Shipping 114, 115, *115*
Shipton, Eric 113
Shiva 87
Shock waves *see* Seismic waves
Shona 101
Short-tailed shearwater 62, *62*
Short-tailed shrew 46
Shrew 43, 46, *55*, 56
Shrike 50, 52, *62*
Shrine 87, 94, 95
Shrubs 46, 54
Shrub wallaby 59
Shwe Dagon Pagoda 93
Siachen glacier 22
Siberia 20, 22, *22*, 116
Siberian ibex 42
Siberian taiga 44, 45, *45*
Siberian tiger 56, *56*
Siberian willow warbler *62*
Sidewinder 52, *53*
Sierra finch 43
Silk 66, *66*
Silkworm 66
Silvered langur *57*
Silver leaf monkey 57
Sinaï 77
Singapore 95, *95*
Sitka spruce 44, *44*
Six-Day War 77, *77*
Skink 53, *53*
Skua 41
Skunk *38*, 46, *47*
Skyscraper 102, 111, *111*
Slavery 34, 76, *76*
Sledge 65
Sloth 55
Sluice gate 29, *29*
Smelting 69
Snake 52, 53, *53*, 54, 56
Snezhnaya Cave 30
Snow 21, 22, 36, 37
Snow goose *62*
Snow house *see* Igloo
Snow leopard 42, *42*
Snowline 36
Snow partridge 42
Snowy owl 41
Sogne Fiord 27
Soil 31
Solomon 86
Somme, battle of 76
Songhai Empire 74, *74*
Song thrush 46
Soubirous, Bernadette 87
Souk 98, *98*
South African veld 49
South America 12, *13*, *24*, *32*, 34, 35, *114*, 117
South American animals 39, *39*, 43, 49, *49*, 52, 55
South-East Asia 26, 35, *39*, 56, 57, 79, *79*, 85, *85*, 117
South-East Trade Wind 24
Southern grey fox 49
South Georgia *32*
South Pole 10, *10*, 36, 38
Soviet Union *see* USSR

Spacecraft 103
Space rocket 69, 103
Spain 72, 74
Spanish ibex 42
Sparrowhawk 46, *47*
Spear 69
Spectacled bear 43, *43*
Spice Islands 73
Spices 73
Spider *54*
Spider monkey *38*, *54*, 55
Spinning wheel 66, *66*
Spire 89
Spitfire *119*
Springbok 51
Spring tide 26
Spruce 44, 88
Spruce mouse 45
Squirrel *39*, 44, 45
Squirrel monkey 55
Sri Lanka 34
Staffa, Isle of 37
Stained glass 89
Stalactite 30
Stalagmite 30
Standard time zones 11
Starboard light 115
Starfish 27
Statue of Liberty 102, *102*
Statue of Zeus 112, *112*
Steinbok 51
Stick insect 54
Stilt house 79, *79*, 95
Stoat 46, *47*
Stone Age 65, 80, *80*, 82, 104, 109, 112
Stone carving 84, 85, 104, *104*, 112, *112*
Stone curlew 52
Stone pine 44, *45*
Stork 50
Straits of Florida 24
Stupa 94, 95
Subduction 12, 25
Sucre 106
Sudan *13*, 34, 79
Suez Canal 100, *114*
Sugar glider 59, *59*
Sugar Loaf Mountain 107
Sulphur 19
Sulphuric acid 33
Sumatra 57
Sumatran rhinoceros *56*
Sumerians 65, 66, 69
Sunshine 20
Sun's rays 10, *10*
Superior, lake 29
Supertanker 114
Surtsey Island 17, *17*
Suryavarman II 85
Suslik 42
Suspension bridge 110, *110*
Swamp *see* Mangrove Swamp
Swan 41
Swallow *62*
Sweetcorn 35
Sweet gum 46
Swiss Alps 111
Swiss Guards 111
Sword 69
Sydney 108, *108*
Sydney Harbour Bridge 108, *108*
Sydney Opera House 108, *108*
Szechwan 43

T
Tabular iceberg 23
Tadzhikistan *110*
Tahr 42
Taiga 44
Taj Mahal 94, *94*
Takahe 61, *61*
Takin 43
Tamandua 55
Tamarack 44
Tamarin *54*, 55

Tambora volcano 17
Tanager 46, *47*, 54
Tanganyika, lake 13, *13*
Tank 76, *76*
Tanker 114
Tanzania 99
Tapeats Sandstone 14
Tapajos *28*
Tapir 43
Tarsier 56
Tasaday people 80, *80*
Tasmania 59, *59*
Tasmanian devil 59, *59*
Tasmanian wolf 59, *59*
Tawny owl 46, *47*
Tayra 55
Tea 34, *34*
Tea ceremony 96, *96*
Tea tax 75
Tegu 54
Tehran 93
Temperate grassland 49
Temperature 20, 38, *38*
Temple 84, 85, 87
Temple of Diana 112, *112*
Temple, The 86
Tenerife 119
Tengmalm's owl *44*
Tent 78, *78*
Tern 41, 62
Terracing 34, 112, *112*
Thailand 95, *95*
Thanksgiving Day 75
Thatched roof 78, 79
Thea sinte 35, *35*
Thebes 94
Thera 113, *113*
Thomson's gazelle 50, *50*, 51
Thrush 46
Thylacine *see* Tasmanian wolf
Tibet 97
Tibetan wild ass 42
Tidal bore 26, *26*
Tidal wave 17
Tide 26
Tierra del Fuego 106, *106*
Tifoultout 98
Tiger 56, *56*
Tiger cat 59, *59*
Tiger shrike *62*
Tilling 68
Timber 78, 94
Timbuktu 74, *74*, 98, *98*
Time zone *11*
Tinamou 49
Tit *45*, 46
Titicaca, lake 29, *29*
Titi monkey 55
Tokyo 96, *96*
Tokyo Bay 96
Tomb 84, 94, *94*, 112, *112*
Tools 69
Topaz hummingbird *54*
Topi 51
Torrent duck 43, *43*
Tortoise 60, *60*
Tortoise moth *47*
Totem pole 105, *105*
Totoro reed 29
Toucan 54, *54*
Tower 91, 95, 98, 115
Tracking station 103
Trade 64, 66, 67, 88, 95, 98, 100
Trade Winds 24
Trains *see* Railway
Trans-Australian railway 108
Transportation 65, 67, 114, 116, *116*, 117, *117*, 118, *118*
Trans-Siberian Railway 116
Tree 44–45, *44–45*, 46, *47*, 49, 54
Treecreeper 46
Tree fern 54
Tree frog 54
Tree groundsel 43

Tree kangaroo 59
Treeless plain 108
Tree pangolin *55*
Tree porcupine 45, 55
Tree shrew *39*
Tree squirrel 45
Trench *see* Ocean trench
Trench warfare 76
Trieste (bathyscaphe) 25
Tristan da Cunha 17, 32, *32*, 62, *62*
Triumphal arch 93, *93*
Trogon 54
Trooping the Colour 89, *89*
Tropical grassland *see* Savannah
Tropical forest 56, *56*
Tropical rain forest 38, *38*, 54, *54*, 55, *55*, *59*
Tropics 20
Tsavo National Park 99, *99*
Tsuki-yama garden 97
Tuareg 82, *82*
Tugela Falls 28
Tulip tree 46
Tundra 38, *38*, 41
Tunnel 111, *111*, 117, *117*
Turbo-jet engine 119
Turbo-prop engine 119
Turkana, lake 13, *13*
Turkey 29, 112, *112*
Turkmenistan *110*
Turks 92
Turnstone 41, *41*
Turtle 63, *63*
Turtle dove 46
Tuscany 90
Tutankhamun 84
Tzu-shi, Chinese empress 76

U
Uakari monkey 55
Uffizi Palace 90
Uganda 99
Ukraine *110*
Underground railway 117
Under-sea features *see* Ocean floor
Union of Soviet Socialist Republics *see* USSR
United Arab Emirates 92
United Nations Building 102
United States of America *see* USA
University 71, *71*
Upfold 36
Ur 69
Uruguay 49
Ural, river 29, *29*
Ural owl 45
Ushaia 106
USA 18, 34, 117
USSR 18, *18*, 29, 110, *110*, 116
Utigard Falls 28
Uzbekistan *110*

V
V2 rocket 69
Valley of the Kings 84, *84*
Vancouver Island 105
Varanasi 87, *87*
Varying hare *45*
Vatican City 86, 111, *111*
Vatican Palace 86, 111
Venezuela 28, 114, *114*
Venice 88, *88*
Venice Simplon Orient Express 116
Verkhoyansk 20
Versailles 89, *89*
Versailles, Treaty of 89
Vervet monkey *39*
Vestiaria coccinea 60
Vesuvius, Mount 18
Victoria, lake 13, *13*, 28
Victoria Falls 101, *101*
Vicuna 29, 43
Vilcabamba 85
Viper 52, 53

Vireo 46, *47*
Virginia deer 38
Virginia opossum 45
Virgin Mary 87
Viscacha 49, *49*
Vishnu 85
Vladivostock 116
Volcano 12, *12*, 13, 16, 17, 18, *18*, 19, 26, 32, 36, 37, 113
Vole 42, 46
Volga, river 29, *29*
Volta, lake 33
Volta, river 33
Vought Corsair *119*
Vulcano Island 17, 19
Vulture 42, 50, *50*

W
Wading birds 41
Wai-'ale-'ale, Mount 21
Wailing Wall 86, *86*
Wallaby 59, *59*
Wallcreeper 42
Walled town 91, 97, 98, 100
Wandering albatross *62*
Warbler 41, 46, 52, *62*
Warfare 69, 76, *76*
Warm current 24, *24*
Warplane 119
Warthog 51
Washington, D.C. 102, *102*
Washington, George *104*
Waste dumping 25
Water chevrotain 55, *55*
Waterfall 28, *28*, 101, *101*
Water shrew 43
Water supply 70, *70*
Water table 31, *31*
Water temperature 52
Water vapour 20, 21
Waterway 70, 88, *88*, 95, *95*, 100, *100*, 103, *103*, 113, 114
Wave Rock 37, *37*
Waxwing 45
Wealth 92
Weapons 69, *69*, 73, *73*
Weasel 41, 46
Weather 20–21, *20–21*
Weaver bird 50, *51*
Weaving *105*
Web-footed water shrew 43
Weddell seal 40
Weka 61, *61*
Well 31, *31*
Welland Canal 103
West Africa 34, 35, 74, *74*
West Asia 78
Westerly Wind 24
Western diamondback rattlesnake *52*
Western Wall *see* Wailing Wall
West Germany 88, *88*
West Wind Drift 24, *24*
Whale 62
Wheatear 41, *62*
Wheel 65, *65*
White-eared puffbird *54*
White-footed mouse 46
White-headed vulture *50*
White House 102, *102*
White Nile, river 28, *28*
White rhinoceros 51, 56
White spruce 44
Whitetail deer 46, *47*
White Volta 33
Wild ass 42, 52
Wild boar *39*, 46, *47*
Wild dog 51
Wildebeest 50, 51
Wild goat 42
Wild sheep 42
Willow 44
Wilson's bird of paradise *58*
Wind 24

Wood block 73
Wolf 45, 46
Wolverine *44*, 45
Wombat 59, *59*
Wooden house 78, *78*, 79, *79*
Woodland *see* Forest
Wood lemming *45*
Wood mouse 46
Woodpecker 46, *47*
Wood pigeon 46
Wood rat 52
Wool 108, *108*
Woolly mammoth 22
Woolly monkey 55
World War I 76, *76*
World War II 76, 77
Worm 46
Wren 46, *52*
Writing 65, *65*, 104, 112

X
Xingu *28*
Xochimilco 104
Xochimilco, lake 104, *104*

Y
Yak *39*, 42, *42*
Yellowhammer 41
Yellow river *see* Hwang-ho river
Yellowstone National Park 37
Yeti 113, *113*
Yoke 68, *68*
Yokohama 96
Yurt 78

Z
Zaire 35
Zaire, river 101
Zambezi, river 101
Zea mays 35, *35*
Zebra 50, *50*, 51
Zen Buddhism 96, 97
Zeus 66
Zeus, Statue of 112, *112*
Zimbabwe 101
Zion Canyon 14
Zuider Zee 32
Zululand 101
Zulus 101, *101*
Zulu War 101

PHOTOGRAPHIC ACKNOWLEDGEMENTS

14 top D. Bridgewater, bottom Geoscience Features; 15 top De Beers, bottom J. Allan Cash Photo Library; 16 top ZEFA, bottom Hawaiian Travel Centre; 17 top Solarfilma, Iceland, bottom BBC Hulton Picture Library; 18 bottom ZEFA; 20 left ZEFA, middle Geoslides, right David and Jill Wright; 21 top ZEFA, bottom Tony Morrison; 22 bottom Geoslides; 25 bottom Israel Tourist Office; 26 top Xinhua News Agency, bottom Paul Popper; 27 top J. Allan Cash Photo Library, bottom ZEFA; 28 bottom ZEFA; 29 bottom ZEFA, top Xinhua News Agency/ZEFA; 30 Photri/ZEFA; 31 top ZEFA, bottom Allan Hutchison; 32 top Royal Netherlands Embassy; 33 left David and Jill Wright, middle Lanecott Co, right J. Allan Cash Photo Library; 36 top ZEFA, bottom ZEFA; 37 top left Institute of Geological Sciences, London, bottom Geoscience Features, top right David and Jill Wright; 64 bottom left Associated press; 73 middle British Library; 77 top BBC Hulton Picture Library, bottom Paul Popper; 80 top J. Nance/J. Hillelson; 84 top ZEFA, middle ZEFA, bottom Italian Ministry of Defence; 85 top ZEFA, middle Geoscience Features, bottom ZEFA; 86 top ZEFA, bottom Jane Taylor/Sonia Halliday; 87 top Dave Collins, bottom left F. H. C. Birch/Sonia Halliday, bottom right ZEFA; 88 bottom J. Allan Cash Photo Library; 89 top ZEFA, bottom left Sonia Halliday; 90 top Italian State Tourist Office, middle ZEFA, bottom ZEFA; 91 top ZEFA, bottom Sonia Halliday; 92 top Sonia Halliday, middle Jane Taylor/Sonia Halliday, bottom ZEFA; 93 top Geoscience Features, middle ZEFA, bottom J. Allan Cash Photo Library; 94 top Dave Collins, middle J. Allan Cash Photo Library; 95 top ZEFA, middle Singapore Tourist Office; 96 bottom Japan Tourist Office; 97 top ZEFA, 98 top left ZEFA, bottom James Wellard/Sonia Halliday; 99 top J. Allan Cash Photo Library, bottom ZEFA; 100 top ZEFA; 101 top C. R. Warn, middle ZEFA; 102 middle B. J. Cruickshank, bottom Geoscience Features; 103 top Space Frontiers, middle Geoscience Features, bottom J. Allan Cash Photo Library; 104 top ZEFA, middle J. Allan Cash Photo Library, bottom British Museum; 105 right ZEFA, left J. Allan Cash Photo Library; 106 top Robert Harding, bottom ZEFA; 107 top ZEFA, bottom ZEFA; 108 Australian News and Information Bureau; 110 top ZEFA; 111 left J. Allan Cash Photo Library, middle ZEFA, right Jane Taylor/Sonia Halliday; 112 bottom right ZEFA; 113 right J. Allan Cash Photo Library; 118 top Saudi Airlines; 119 top Central Press Photos.

Picture research: Jackie Cookson